Norse
Myths

To Anne-Margrethe Hustad

THE · LEGENDARY · PAST

Norse
Myths

R. I. PAGE

Published for the
Trustees of the British Museum by
BRITISH MUSEUM PUBLICATIONS

Published by British Museum Publications Ltd
46 Bloomsbury Street, London WC1B 3QQ

British Library Cataloguing in Publication Data
Page, R. I. (Raymond Ian), 1924–
    Norse myths. – (The legendary past).
    1. Scandinavian tales and legends
    I. Title II. Series
    398.20948
    ISBN 0-7141-2062-6

Designed by Gill Mouqué
Cover design by Slatter-Anderson

Set in 10½ pt Sabon and printed in Great Britain
by The Bath Press, Avon

THIS PAGE *Pagan Viking burial stones at Lindholm Høje, Jutland, Denmark. The stones are set in the shape of ships.*

Contents

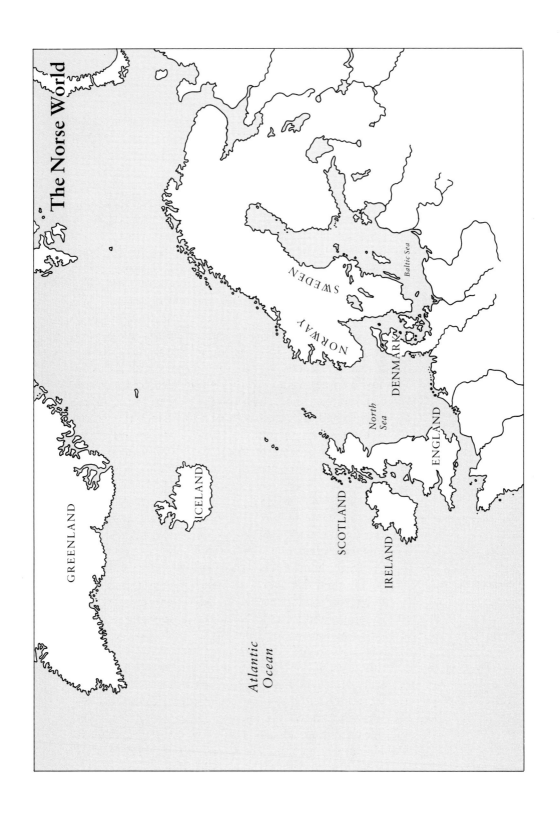

The Norse World

GREENLAND

ICELAND

Atlantic
Ocean

SCOTLAND

IRELAND

ENGLAND

North
Sea

DENMARK

NORWAY

SWEDEN

Baltic Sea

Introduction

A myth, says the *Oxford English Dictionary* profoundly, is 'a purely fictitious narrative usually involving supernatural persons, actions, or events, and embodying some popular idea concerning natural or historical phenomena'; it adds more cheerfully that the word is often used vaguely 'to include any narrative having fictitious elements'. In this book I use 'myth' neither as loosely as in the second of these definitions nor as rigorously as in the first. Certainly most of the tales retold here deal with supernatural persons and actions, and so provide a guide to pagan Norse thinking as reported by medieval writers. But not all the stories are purely fictitious. Some of those in the final chapter, treating of battle, murder and sudden death in a heroic society, have an origin in historical event, though distant. However, most chapters contain myths of the gods and goddesses of pagan Viking Scandinavia. Some of these clearly embody ideas about natural phenomena (and hence, I suppose, the reason for their creation); these are likely to appeal to readers engaged in modern cults of mysticism. Other stories may also have done this, but they are opaque, and I, not being an anthropologist or folklorist, can only guess at what the ideas were. Others again look to us now like tales told for pleasure, and that is presumably what most modern readers will take them as.

From the records that survive it is clear that the Norsemen had many gods and goddesses. Some of them are hardly known to us, as Ull, splendid archer, ski-champion and fighter, and Var, the goddess 'who takes note of oaths and specific agreements made between men and women . . . and wreaks vengeance on people who break them'. Such deities are little more than names to modern readers, though in their day they, like their fellow-gods, may have had myths told of them. Inevitably, however, the body of this book records the myths of the great gods and goddesses of Scandinavia, though we should always keep in mind that what survives may be only a small, and is certainly a random, sample of what once existed.

Best known are the gods of the race of Aesir, one of the two main groups of gods in the Norse pantheon. Leading them is **Odin**, universal father, god of poetic inspiration, of mystery and magic, patron of warriors. He was married to **Frigg**, goddess who knows the fates of all men. Other gods are often referred to as Odin's children. First is **Thor**, a warrior god, defender of the Aesir against their natural enemies, the giants. He married **Sif** about whom little is known save that her hair was of gold. Other sons of Odin

A runic memorial stone from Hanning, Denmark, whose inscription ends (top left) with a hammer symbol which some have seen as a reference to Thor, although its late date, 12th century, could make it a tradesman's sign.

A one-eyed figure (left), identified as Odin on the ground that Odin is the only important one-eyed figure in Scandinavian mythology. He is said to have given an eye in return for understanding.

are **Bragi**, god of eloquence and poetry, married to the important goddess **Idunn** who kept the apples of eternal youth; and the handsome but unfortunate **Baldr**, married to **Nanna**, and who was killed by accident by the blind god **Hod**. Also defined as Odin's son is **Tyr**, the brave and wise god of war who lost his hand in helping to fetter the dread wolf Fenrir. A more mysterious figure is **Heimdall**, watchman and herald of the final battle that ends the life of the gods in this world. He is the foe of **Loki**, a baffling figure, part god and part demon, who was son of a giant Farbauti, and married to the devoted Sigyn. However, he also had issue by a giantess Angrboda, and they turned out to be sinister indeed: the wolf Fenrir, the World Serpent Iormungand and the supernatural creature who presided over the other world, Hel.

Side by side with the Aesir live a group of gods of the race of Vanir, deities of fertility and wealth. These are Niord, Freyr and Freyia. **Niord** is god of seafaring, fishing and riches. He married a giantess Skadi, but they could not agree. Niord's children are the twins **Freyr** and **Freyia**, who also mated together. Freyr married a giantess Gerd, and Freyia a character called Od. Freyr and Freyia control fertility and produce.

There are also a number of minor deities, Hoenir, Kvasir, Gefion, Vali, Vili, Ve, Vidar and so on, as well as a variety of other supernatural creatures below the rank of gods: dwarfs, elves, norns, witches, valkyries. But the gods' greatest enemies are the *iotnar* (singular *iotunn*), a word usually translated 'giants'; for these ancient, ugly, terrible and usually ill-intentioned creatures something like 'demons' or 'trolls' would be equally apposite.

In the translations in this book I have sought to be fluent rather than faithful to the original in every detail. This is particularly the case in the verse translations, where I have tried to make sense while keeping roughly to the lineation of the primary texts. There will always be some arbitrariness in rendering Old Norse names (and other words) in modern English prose, and I admit this in the present work. In the main, if I give a name or word in italics, it will be in the 'standard' Old Norse/Icelandic form. This will sometimes contain unusual letter forms, of which the most important are þ and ð which Norse uses for the various sounds that modern English represents by *th*. Otherwise, if the name is in Roman in continuous prose, it will be an adaptation of the standard form, without inflexional ending or accent and perhaps with some adaptation like d for ð: as Odin in the place of *Óðinn*. This will raise occasional problems when I quote Latinised forms, as Othinus instead of Odin, or Frothi for Frodi (*Fróði*). Occasionally I have completely anglicised a name or nickname: it seems absurd, for instance, to speak of Eirik blodox (*Eiríkr blóðøx*) rather than Eric Bloodaxe.□

Miniature gold foils from Norway. Some have interpreted these scenes as Freyr and Gerd, for no compelling reason.

Where to find Norse myths

Mention the word 'Norsemen' and the English will think first of the Vikings, those enterprising and ruthless peoples who, in the three centuries from 800 to 1100, plundered, colonised, conquered, traded with, developed and sometimes even civilised countries east and west of Scandinavia. That these people had a pagan religion, and with it a pagan mythology of some complexity, is without doubt. How much of either can be recovered is less clear. The Vikings were illiterate save for their inscriptions, so they recorded little of their beliefs and still less of their myths. Any knowledge of these that we now have comes either from outside Scandinavia if within the Viking Age, or from within Scandinavia in the post-Viking era. Extra-Scandinavian material was written down by Christians unsympathetic to Viking ideas, beliefs and behaviour, and so is sparse. Later Scandinavian writings may derive from Viking sources, but it is difficult to know how precisely and accurately; and their expression is often affected by ways of thinking and writing that are common European and Christian.

Christianity established itself quite late in mainland Scandinavia. In Denmark there was a strong and authoritative move towards the new religion in the mid-tenth century. Norway was a little later, the end of the tenth and the first decades of the eleventh. Sweden was later still. The Icelanders, if their medieval historians were well informed, formally adopted Christianity about the year 1000. Viking colonists elsewhere may have become Christians earlier, though still late by Western European standards. The Norse settlers of East Anglia issued a coinage commemorating the Christian sainthood of King Edmund a couple of decades after they martyred him in 870. The colonisers of the Isle of Man were putting up memorial crosses in the tenth century; by then they were intermarrying with the native Christian Celts.

Of course, we need not assume that the advent of Christianity necessarily made radical changes in Norse practice or belief. It was quite possible, we are told, for an Irish Norseman to put his trust in both Christ and Thor. Rather than replace it, the Christian myth may have been added to, or may have penetrated Norse myth. The great eleventh-century cross in the churchyard of Gosforth, Cumbria, has its carved crucifixion scene, but also other sculptures interpreted as illustrations of Norse myths of the gods. At Andreas, Isle of Man, is a cross-slab fragment bearing, below one of the cross arms, the figure of a spear-carrying man savaged by a beast, apparently the god Odin attacked by the dread wolf Fenrir.

A soapstone mould for both the pagan and the Christian – Thor's hammer and Christ's cross could be produced.

The wolf Fenrir attacks Odin at Ragnarok. One of Odin's ravens perches nonchalantly on his shoulder. From a memorial stone at Andreas, Isle of Man.

Amulet in the shape of Thor's hammer, worn as a pendant. From Rømersdal, Denmark.

For contemporary records of Viking myth, then, we go not to texts but to carvings; or to miniatures like the hammer-head amulets which occur from time to time in Viking contexts and indicate that stories of the hammer-bearing god Thor were already current; or, much less certainly, to a small group of figurines, which some have thought to be statuettes of gods with their characteristic attributes but others, more mundanely, have considered to be playing-pieces for some board game or other. If we want elaborated versions of the myths, however, we have to get them from the medieval Scandinavia of the post-Viking era, with all the problems of corruption and inaccuracy that this later provenance brings with it.

Poetic Edda

Our knowledge depends on three major sources. The first is the *Poetic Edda*, a group of loosely related texts, poems of a short or middle length. The heart of this collection fills a manuscript called the *Codex Regius*, the Royal Manuscript, so named because it was a treasure of the Royal Library at Copenhagen for centuries before it returned to its native land in 1971, following an agreement between the Danish and Icelandic governments. The *Codex Regius* is a vellum manuscript written in the second half of the thirteenth century, nearly three hundred years after Iceland's conversion to Christianity. It contains twenty-nine poems, eleven of them on mythological topics, sixteen, together with two fragments, on heroes and heroines of Germanic antiquity. There are other manuscripts preserving a few poems of a similar form and nature, while verse quotations in prose texts are evidence of yet more, now lost save for what is quoted. In effect we retain a random sample of a verse literature of unknown size, a fact that must always be in our minds when we try to draw conclusions from what survives.

Moreover, though it is comparatively easy to say where and when the *Codex Regius* was written, it is fearsomely difficult, perhaps impossible, to determine where and when the Eddic poems themselves were composed. Casually the *Codex Regius* brings together works from different dates and lands. Some of the poems may go back to the early years of the Viking Age; others may be as late as the twelfth century when Scandinavian civilisation had moved into the European Middle Ages. Some may be from Norway, others from the western settlements, perhaps from Ireland or Greenland.

The Eddic verses are more or less stanzaic, with a limited degree of metrical variation, so they present quite a homogeneous appearance. Yet the mythological poems differ a good deal in content and treatment. Some are narrative as a ballad is narrative, with a sequence of quickly changing scenes interspersed with direct speech to recount adventures of the gods. Others are question-and-answer poems, dialogues between supernatural beings serving to display mythological information. Occasionally there is a series of stanzas containing traditional wisdom or proverb attributed to one of the deities. All these reveal much of the Norse picture of their gods, but often allusively so that a listener must apply knowledge he already has to illuminate a chance reference.

An example is one of the simplest of narrative poems, *Þrymskviða*, the tale of the giant-king Thrym. It opens with Thor waking in his bed and reaching for the mighty hammer that gives him power and security. It is gone, stolen. He must find it or the giants will invade the land of the gods and destroy them. His crony Loki, a deity whose qualities vary from the

A silver pendant from Iceland, with an animal-head thong hole, that may represent either Christ's cross or Thor's hammer.

cheeky and mischievous to the evil, is with him. Together they go to the home of the lovely goddess Freyia and ask for her skin of feathers so that one of them may fly over the earth in search of the hammer. Freyia gladly lends it. Loki puts on the skin and flies from Asgard (Godland) to the realm of the giants. He chances on Thrym, who boasts he has hidden the hammer and will not return it until the gods send him Freyia as his bride. Loki reports back to Thor and together they go to the home of the lovely Freyia – there is ballad-style repetition of wording here – and tell her to get a wedding dress on at once as she must go to Iotunheim (Giantland) as Thrym's bride:

> Freyia was furious, in wrath she snorted,
> The hall of the great gods shook beneath her.
> Her glittering necklace shot in pieces.
> 'Am I so mad to get a man
> That I'd drive with you to Iotunheim!'

The gods call a hasty meeting and one of them, the far-seeing Heimdall, has an inspiration. Let Thor dress up in women's clothes and drive to Iotunheim, pretending to be Freyia.

> Brawniest of gods, Thor then spoke:
> 'The gods will think that I've gone gay
> If I have to wear a wedding dress.'

The gods overcome his objections, dress him up and send him to Iotunheim with Loki disguised as his lady's maid. Thrym and the giants are, surprisingly, taken in, but Thor nearly gives the game away at the wedding feast by wolfing down and drinking up so much that Thrym is horror-struck at his bride's voracious appetite. Only Loki's quick wit saves them; he excuses 'Freyia', saying she is so infatuated with Thrym that she has not been able to touch a morsel of food for days beforehand. Thrym is eager to hurry the wedding along, and orders up the sacred hammer to bless the bride with. The moment Thor sees the hammer his heart exults. He grabs it, and flattens all the giant race. So he gets his hammer back.

    The tale is wittily and broadly told. It is funny even to anyone with no previous knowledge of the Norse gods. But Freyia's wrath is funnier if you know she is the goddess of fertility and sexual love, who is notoriously 'mad to get a man'. It also helps to know something of Norse moral attitudes. Thor's horror at wearing drag is the more piquant because effeminacy in a man filled the Vikings with loathing, and Thor was aggressively tough and virile, even if not very bright. When you see the force of the jokes, you are driven to the question: what sort of poet could write such verses? We do not know their date, save that it was before the end of the thirteenth century. Could a pagan have jested like this about his gods, amused at them while relying on their support? Or is the poem the work of a mocking Christian who despised these false deities? If the latter, is this a genuine tale from Norse mythology, or is it a made-up thing, composed to throw scorn on the old faith? The debate continues.

Again, there is the case of the poem called *Hávamál*, the Chant of the High One. This is a complex work, made up of a number of individual stanza sequences which were collected together under the single heading at some early date. When is a matter of controversy. Some would have it this is a chance selection of ancient verses linked by the personality of the great god Odin, the High One himself. Others interpret it as a learned compilation and edition from perhaps the twelfth century. In either case most scholars accept that *Hávamál* incorporates matter of great antiquity, probably from the Viking Age: it tells something of the Viking world-picture.

Much of the poem is in proverbial mode, useful if rather down-to-earth advice on how to lead your life. There is talk of friendship, its obligations and benefits, of the duties of hospitality, of the importance of caution, keeping your wits about you, of poverty and its troubles, of whom you can trust and whom you can't, of the need to be well thought of, and so on – all subjects appropriate to a god of worldly wisdom. There is magical material, chants and spells, suited to a god of magic. And there is the occasional narrative sequence. Immediately after a group of wisdom stanzas addressed to an unknown Loddfafnir, immediately before a catalogue of magical practices that someone, presumably Odin, has mastered, are a couple of baffling verses:

> I mind I hung on the windswept tree
> Nine whole nights,
> Stabbed by the spear, given to Odin,
> Myself to myself.
> Of that tree no man knows
> What roots it springs from.

> No bread they gave me, no drink from the horn,
> Down I peered.
> I took up runes, howling I took them up,
> And back again I fell.

This is weird stuff indeed. The hearers must have understood the circumstances (though of course if this is a chance-preserved gobbet of a longer poem, the original may have given more detail), but what were they? Nowhere else in Norse literature, I think, survives any version of this myth, so we must guess at its meaning and context. It seems to represent something like a shamanistic test Odin took upon himself in order to learn esoteric magic, that of the runic letters. There are things in Norse record that match some of its details. We know that at the great temple of Uppsala, Sweden, beasts and men hung from the trees of the sacred grove, sacrifices to the gods. We know Odin was nicknamed 'God of the Hanged'. We know the spear was his special weapon. We know he had skills in runes and that this strange script was believed to give access to supernatural powers. But we have no surviving story about Odin that confirms this short and cryptic passage of *Hávamál*. Moreover, as it is related here, the tale shows disturbing similarities to the Christian myth: Christ hanging on the cross-beam, pierced by a spear, tormented by thirst, achieving the fullness of his Godhead by his willing self-sacrifice. Were there two myths here, perhaps ultimately related? Or did one invade the world of the other?

A third example is from the poem *Lokasenna*, Loki Quarrelling. Here Loki is the evil one, excluded from the company of the other gods and goddesses. They give a party and Loki is not invited. So he pushes his way in and engages in unseemly banter with each of those present. Each indelicate allusion – by Loki or his opponent – takes up one stanza. For example, when the god Tyr interposes to defend one of his fellows:

> Loki said:
> 'Shut up, Tyr. You were never fit
> To reconcile two foes.
> Let me mention that right hand of yours
> That Fenrir tore away.'
>
> Tyr said:
> 'So I've lost a hand. You've lost Hrodrsvitnir.
> Each suffers sorrowful loss.
> The wolf too is wretched; he must wait
> Enchained till the world's end.'

Here I have quoted practically all that *Lokasenna* relates of this myth, yet the audience must have known more of it or the verses would make no sense to them. We are lucky to know the whole tale, for Snorri Sturluson (1179–1241) wrote a detailed summary in his *Prose Edda*. In two separate passages Snorri told of Tyr's encounter with the ferocious wolf Fenrir, who seems in *Lokasenna* to have also the name or nickname of Hrodrsvitnir. Tyr, said Snorri, was the boldest of the gods, the patron of brave warriors. The wolf Fenrir was one of the monstrous brood of Loki, born to a giant woman. The gods heard a prophecy that the wolf and his kin would one day destroy the world, so they seized the beast to be brought up under their control. Only Tyr had the courage to tend him. Things were quiet while the wolf was a cub, but when the gods saw how huge he was growing they got anxious and decided to chain him up. How to put the chain on? They tried to trick the wolf (and it is worth noting that treachery and cunning were part of the gods' moral code). They persuaded him to let himself be fettered, pretending it was a test of his strength to get out; the tougher the chain, the greater the prestige in breaking it. Unfortunately, however strong the fetter, the wolf shattered it.

The only answer was to get those skilled craftsmen, the dwarfs, to make a custom-built chain, from six elements: the sound of a cat prowling, a woman's beard, a mountain's root, a bear's sinews, a fish's breath and a bird's spittle, all things with little or no physical entity. The dwarfs accepted the commission. Not surprisingly, from these materials they produced a very slender chain indeed, but one immensely strong for all that. Then the gods tried to trick the wolf into putting it on, arguing that anyone who could destroy iron bands would easily break out of this. But their own casuistry defeated them, for the wolf retorted there was no prestige in snapping such a slim chain unless it had been made with guile, and in that case he wanted nothing to do with it. Eventually, however, fearing that his courage would be questioned, Fenrir agreed but only on condition that, as a pledge of good faith, one of the gods should put his hand into the wolf's jaws while he was chained up. The gods looked at one another in perplexity. None wanted this office. At last the brave Tyr accepted it. They fettered the wolf with the deceitful chain. He struggled to escape, could not, and bit off Tyr's hand. 'Then they all laughed – except Tyr.'

The gods took Fenrir and tied him to a rock with a sword wedged between his jaws to stop him biting. They left him there, and *þar liggr hann til ragnarøkrs*, 'there he lies until the end of the world'.

Prose Edda

This tale introduces us to the second of the great collections of mythological material, the *Prose Edda*. Snorri Sturluson was a very rich Icelandic farmer, local leader, territorial magnate, ambassador, and something of a quisling in the service of the imperialistic Norwegian king, Hakon Hakonarson. Withal he was an educated man, having an unmatched knowledge of his country's antiquities and literature. He was himself a poet, and compiled his *Prose Edda* in the 1220s as a handbook of mythology for budding poets.

The book falls into four sections: a prologue; *Gylfaginning*, Fooling Gylfi; *Skáldskaparmál*, the Diction of Poetry; and *Háttatal*, the List of Verse Forms. The last is the least relevant to our subject: a series of definitions, with technical descriptions and examples, of the various and complex forms of line and stanza used by early Norse court poets. The first three sections belong more coherently together. Their purpose is explained in a passage from *Skáldskaparmál*, addressing young poets 'who want to learn poetic diction and to get themselves a wide vocabulary of traditional terms, or who want to be able to follow what is expressed elliptically in verse'. Snorri's book is an explication of the mythological allusions common in traditional verse, to help newcomers to the art to get them right. These poets of the thirteenth century would have been Christians, yet their verses were expected to abound in references to a pagan mythology that had been dead, more or less, for over two hundred years. Without instruction they might make mistakes.

To take an example. If your poem had to mention gold, you could refer to it as 'Frodi's meal'. It would then be helpful to know of the mythical king Frodi of Denmark, who had a quern that would grind out whatever its owner asked for. Frodi wanted gold, and kept his mill-slaves Fenia and Menia toiling day and night grinding out wealth for him. Or you could call gold 'Kraki's seed' in a reference to the legendary Danish king Hrolf Kraki. Chased by an avenging enemy, he scattered his golden plunder behind him as a sower broadcasts seed. If you had not these stories in mind, you might mistakenly call gold 'the seed of Frodi' or 'the meal of Kraki'. To give a modern parallel. Recently I heard a radio chat-show in which the hostess interviewed a famous guest who had radically changed his career in mid-life. She asked: 'Did you come to do this after careful thought? Or did you see, as it were, a blinding light on the road to Emmaus?' Had she had access to a modern Christian equivalent of Snorri's *Edda*, or even had she read the *Acts of the Apostles*, she might not have confused the road to Emmaus with the road to Damascus.

But Snorri too was a Christian, and could hardly tell such tales as though they were the truth, particularly tales that related adventures of the pagan gods. So he distanced himself from his subject in a number of ways. He composed a prologue full of early anthropological observation: how in primitive times men realised there was order in the universe, and deduced it must have a ruler; how the most splendid of early communities was Troy in Turkey, with twelve kingdoms each with a prince of superhuman qualities, and one high king above all. Snorri traced one of these royal dynasties to a son called Tror: 'we call him Thor'. Thor went out adventuring, met up with a beautiful witch called Sibil, 'whom we call Sif', and by her spawned a race full of the names of great heroes and one in particular, Odin. Odin had supernatural powers (as did his wife Frigg), for which he knew his name would 'be honoured beyond all kings'. He left Asia and travelled north, setting his sons in charge of kingdoms there, organising communities on the Trojan pattern. From these incomers from Asia (who were hence called *Aesir*, which is the common Old Norse word for 'gods') descended the great kings of Scandinavia. Here Snorri has taken an orthodox Christian position, identifying the pagan gods as ancient heroes deified by their ignorant followers.

The first part proper of Snorri's *Edda*, *Gylfaginning*, sets its material in a narrative frame. Gylfi was a Swedish king, something of a philosopher. He was perplexed by the Aesir, since all things seemed to work according to their will. Were they gods, or did they get their power from gods whom they worshipped? He set off to find out, disguised as a tramp, Gangleri. But the Aesir spotted him coming and prepared an illusion for him; hence this section's title, 'Fooling Gylfi'. When he came to the land of the Aesir, he saw an enormous hall which turned out to be full of people disporting themselves. At one end were three thrones, each occupied by a king: the first king was called High, the second Just-as-High, the third simply Third. These august rulers were prepared to answer Gylfi's questions. He asked about the gods and received in reply encyclopaedic lore, folk-tale, legend. By this device Snorri was able to tell his myths through intermediaries, not committing himself to their truth. He could also tell them in a detached, witty, drily ironical style which is a joy to read.

Some of his material Snorri certainly had from poems like those of the *Poetic Edda*, though they may not have been identical with the ones that have come down to us. As evidence for what he writes, he sometimes quotes passages from verses represented in the *Codex Regius*, as here in a passage telling of the great warriors whom Odin picks from the battlefield and takes

Gangleri questions the three kings: High, Just-as-High and Third.

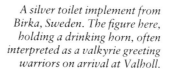

A silver toilet implement from Birka, Sweden. The figure here, holding a drinking horn, often interpreted as a valkyrie greeting warriors on arrival at Valholl.

to live with him in his great hall of Valholl. Snorri makes High say:

Every day when they have got up, they put on their war-gear and go out into the arena and fight, each pouncing on the other. This is their idea of sport. And when dinner-time approaches, they ride home to Valholl and sit down at their drink; as it says in this verse:

> All the great champions
> In Odin's circle
> Battle together each day.
> They choose who shall die,
> Ride from the fight,
> And sit together in peace again.

The verse occurs in just this form in the question-and-answer poem *Vafþrúð nismál* in the *Codex Regius*.

But Snorri also makes it clear that he knew poems that have not survived independently: witness his story of Niord, god of sea travel and mercantile adventure, who made a *mésalliance* with the giantess Skadi and had to compromise on living conditions.

Skadi wanted to live where her father had lived, in the hills called Thrymheim. On the other hand Niord wanted to live near the sea. So they came to an agreement that they should stay in turns, nine days at Thrymheim and the next nine at Noatun [Niord's seaside residence]. And when Niord came back to Noatun from the hills he proclaimed this verse:

> I'm bored with the hills, I didn't stay long
> Nine nights only.
> Wolves' howling I hated
> Compared with swans' singing.

And Skadi said:

> I couldn't sleep by the ocean's beds
> For the sea-bird's screaming.
> Every dawn it wakens me,
> The gull flying in from the sea.

So Skadi went to the hills and lived in Thrymheim. She usually wears skis and carries a bow for shooting animals. And she is known as the ski-ing goddess.

The verses are known only from Snorri's *Edda* but must derive from a full-length poem now lost.

In other cases again we have no clear idea where Snorri got his story from, though the amount of detail he gives shows he had full sources which may have been folk-tale or tradition. To this group perhaps belongs the tale of how the gods planned a defensive wall round their territory to guard it from giant attack. They found a builder who, though they did not realise it at the time, was of giant kin. He agreed to construct the wall for a fee: the sun, the moon and the goddess Freyia. He was allowed no help save from his cart-horse Svadilfoeri, and he had to finish the job in three seasons or he would lose everything. Thor was not at home when this was arranged, but Loki was, and he advised the gods to accept the contract, thinking the task was impossible. The gods agreed, and bound themselves by oaths to keep the bargain.

The builder worked all day, and by night brought out his horse to fetch stones. When the gods saw the horse at work they were horrified to find how much it could pull at a load – it worked twice as hard even as the builder! Time was nearly up, the wall practically complete. The gods were terrified they would lose, and assailed Loki, blaming him for his bad advice. Loki in turn was frightened, and devised a plot to stop the builder from winning. He turned himself into a mare. On the last night the builder drove his horse to get the final load of materials; out popped the mare and whinnied at the horse, which went frantic and broke its traces, trying to get at its mate. The two galloped away to the woods and were absent all night, so the builder could not get his task finished. At that he fell into a giant rage, and this made the gods realise at last that he was of enemy kin. At the critical moment Thor came home and saw the danger. He swung his mighty hammer, smashing the giant's skull in splinters. But the last laugh was on Loki. He gave birth to a monstrous foal with eight legs. This grew into the famous horse Sleipnir, which was Odin's favourite mount.

As evidence for this tale, Snorri quotes two verses from the great Eddic poem *Vǫluspá*, The Wise Woman's Prophecy. They are quite inadequate to explain the detail that Snorri's version contains. So, either he made up the

This design, incised on a stone in Gotland, Sweden, shows an eight-legged horse, usually assumed to represent Odin's favourite mount Sleipnir.

21

whole tale himself – and this is unlikely – or he had some source that we cannot trace.

The second part proper of Snorri's *Edda, Skáldskaparmál*, also has a narrative frame. Again there is a visitor to the Aesir, who again are not identified as gods though they have the same names as gods. This visitor is Aegir, a king skilled in magic. Again the Aesir spot him in advance and prepare both reception and deception. They give him a great welcome and prepare a feast in his honour, sitting him next to Bragi whose name is that of the god of poetry. Bragi tells of the exploits of the Aesir. So the traditional myths are expounded, ending with a very important one for Snorri's purpose. This tells of two dwarfs, Fialar and Galar, who killed a creature Kvasir and mixed his blood with honey, so making the mead that turns anyone who drinks it into a poet. The dwarfs kept their mead in three cauldrons. A giant, Suttung, took it from them, and Odin in his turn plotted to steal it. He seduced the giant's daughter who was so infatuated that she let him take three drinks of the mead, which completely emptied the cauldrons. Then Odin turned himself into an eagle and flew off over the mountains. When Suttung discovered his loss, he put on his own eagle skin and rose in pursuit, nearly catching Odin up. The Aesir saw Odin's peril as he hovered over their dwellings, so they quickly put out into the courtyard all their pails and jars. Odin spewed up the mead into them, and there it remains, waiting to be distributed to anyone who aspires to be a poet. Thus, says Snorri (or perhaps Bragi), poetry can be called 'Odin's plunder' or 'Odin's discovery' or 'Odin's drink'.

Here Snorri has got to the main purpose of writing his *Edda*: a discussion of the language and imagery of poetry, how its metaphors can be understood in terms of Norse mythology. Now the narrative frame of *Skáldskaparmál* recedes into the background, and Snorri is content to ask questions. Why is gold referred to as 'the hair of Sif', or as 'the otter's blood-money', or as 'Aegir's fire'? And he gives the stories that explain the images. Or he tells of the appropriate metaphors to be used of the various gods: 'How do you refer to Tyr? By calling him "the one-handed god", "the wolf's feeder".' We know why: Snorri told us the story in *Gylfaginning*. 'How do you refer to Hod? By calling him "the blind god", "Baldr's killer", "shooter of the mistletoe",' referring to the Baldr tragedy, a most important myth which I discuss later. This type of metaphor, *kenning* as it is named in Old Norse, may be a myth in shorthand. It is an essential feature of Norse court poetry.

Skaldic verse

This introduces naturally the third of our major sources for Norse myth, the compositions of the court poets, the skalds as they are usually called. The *Poetic Edda* is anonymous; in contrast, many skaldic verses are attributed to named poets. Their biographies may be preserved or their political allegiances known. Moreover, their verses often refer to contemporary events which can be dated on independent evidence. Thus with skaldic verse it is possible to build up a chronology of writings, to date many of the poems at any rate to within a decade or so. The practice of composing skaldic verse began perhaps in the ninth century and continued through the Viking Age into the Middle Ages; but of course, save for occasional stanzas cut in runes, little of it was written down until the advent of Christianity and Roman literacy. So we have the familiar problem. We have to trust to Christian records of a pre- or proto-Christian era. We have to assume accurate oral transmission of verse until the period of writing down. And we have to accept that the later attribution of verses to named poets is sound. Using skaldic verse as evidence is clearly perilous.

Skaldic poetry was usually highly mannered and technically elaborate, as befits a form of verse designed for songs in praise of Scandinavian kings and nobles. It could also be the vehicle for occasional verse, to celebrate great occasions or simply for impromptu comment on happenings the poet observed or took part in. As well as a complex verse form, most skaldic poems had a complex language pattern with sentences intermingled and employing unusual words in place of common ones, and making frequent use of kennings. It is in these kennings that myths may be concealed.

For instance, the poet Einar Skalaglamm composed a poem, *Vellekla*, in honour of the great earl Hakon of Lade, near Trondheim in Norway, towards the end of the tenth century. He opened it with a formal request to his patron for a hearing:

> Great-hearted land's protector,
> I beg you to listen to the yeasty surf
> Of the dwellers of the fiord's bone.
> Hear, earl, Kvasir's blood.

On its first performance, the listeners must have scratched their heads a bit at this until they managed to work out the various periphrases. 'Kvasir's blood' is easy enough when you know it was made into mead, a special sort of mead that gives poetic inspiration; hence the kenning can be used for a specific example of poetic inspiration, an individual poem. 'The yeasty surf of the dwellers of the fiord's bone' is trickier, more involved. 'The fiord's bone' is the rocky shore or cliff of a fiord. 'The dwellers of the fiord's bone' are, or at least may be, dwarfs, since every schoolboy knows that dwarfs live in crags or great boulders. Here the dwarfs are Fialar and Galar. Their 'yeasty surf' would be their mead; hence again we have a kenning for poetry, a poem. All the poet has said in these lines is 'Please be quiet and listen while I'm reciting', but it sounds more impressive this way. However, it does depend on audience participation: if they cannot remember the myth and unravel the riddle, they will be baffled by the verse.

Luckily, not all skaldic verse is as hard to follow as this. Some skalds wrote comparatively straightforward verse, while still exploiting mythological thought patterns. When the great tenth-century Icelandic poet Egil Skalla-grimsson lost two of his sons, he composed a bitter lament scolding his patron, the poet's god Odin, for betraying him. It was hard to compose in such circumstances, he said. 'It is not a propitious time for the theft of Vidrir.' Vidrir is another name for Odin; his theft was the mead of poetry. But though Odin had injured him, he had also, by his gift of poetry, strengthened Egil. 'If I look upon things properly, Mimir's friend has brought me recompense for my grief.' Mimir was Odin's friend because his wise head, cut off and pickled, told Odin many secrets about the future.

Again, a skald might praise his lord in an almost Eddic form, writing a simple narrative verse in a scene set amongst the gods. When Eric Bloodaxe, exiled king of both Norway and York, came to grief in battle in the mid-tenth century, his fiercely pagan wife commissioned an appropriate funeral ode. Only a few verses of it survive. They begin in Odin's hall:

> Odin said:
> 'What dream was that? I rose at dawn
> To clear Valholl for a slaughtered army.
> I roused my great champions; bade the Valkyries wake,
> Strew the benches, wash out the beer-mugs,
> Bring out the wine for a prince who was coming.
> From earth I am looking for
> Such noble fighting-men
> As will make my heart exult.'

He asks his companion Bragi what the thunderous noise outside is. Bragi thinks it is the god Baldr returning home. Odin tells him not to be daft; it's obviously Eric and the army of the dead who have been killed with him. He sends out his two greatest heroes to welcome the king. One of them, Sigmund, heroic but not unduly intelligent, asks why Odin expects Eric rather than someone else. Odin explains patiently that Eric is a great warrior: 'because he has reddened his sword, carried a bloody blade, in many lands'. Sigmund asks reasonably: 'If he seemed so valiant, why rob him of victory?' Odin makes the veiled reply:

> 'What's to come cannot be known.
> The grey wolf glares at the homes of the gods.'

Eric was a fairly mediocre king, unsuccessful in most of his ventures. By treating him like this the poet has shown him as one of the greatest fighters, fit to mix with the heroes of antiquity, fit to form part of Odin's defending army when the grey wolf Fenrir escapes his bonds and takes ferocious vengeance on the gods.

In some cases mythological tales may be more directly the subject of a skald's verses. An example is the poem *Haustlǫng*, Autumn-long, so called because it took its writer Thiodolf a whole autumn to finish. The poem describes a shield the skald had been given, decorated with a group of scenes portraying a couple of stories of the gods. One told the tale of Idunn, a useful goddess since she kept in a chest the apples that gave renewed youth. Snorri, who knew *Haustlǫng*, tells her story plainly.

Three of the Aesir, Odin, Loki and Hoenir, were on an expedition, and one day seized and killed an ox for supper. They tried to cook it, but whenever they checked the meat was not ready. Above them was an oak, and in its branches an eagle. The eagle revealed it was responsible for the cooking failure; the beef would never be done unless the eagle got its share. The gods accepted this and invited the bird to help itself. So it did, too freely for Loki's taste. Loki was furious, picked up a staff and beat at the eagle. The staff stuck to the eagle which flew off, with Loki, who was also stuck to the staff, hanging on behind. Loki, shaken and battered, was terrified and pleaded to be let loose. The eagle agreed on condition that Loki promised to entice Idunn out of her stronghold among the gods, bringing her apples with her. So Loki and the others got home safely.

Loki faithfully kept his bargain, luring Idunn out into the woods. The eagle, now revealed as a giant Thiazi, swooped upon her and carried her off to his home in Thrymheim. The gods, apple-less, began to grow old and feeble. They were puzzled at what had happened to Idunn until someone remembered she had last been seen with Loki. So they arrested Loki and threatened him with death unless he found Idunn and brought her back. Loki transformed himself into a hawk and flew off to Thrymheim. Luckily the giant was out fishing and Idunn at home alone. Loki turned her into a nut, picked her up in his talons and flew off. Thiazi, finding Idunn gone, put on his eagle shape and went off in pursuit, flapping so violently that his wings caused tempests. The Aesir saw the hawk struggling, chased by an eagle, and realised the situation. They heaped up a pile of woodchips just inside their walls, and when the hawk had flown safely in, they lit the wood. The eagle was flying so violently it could not stop. Into the fire it went and its wings were destroyed. The Aesir killed Thiazi.

Snorri has a sequel to this tale. Thiazi had a butch daughter called Skadi. When she heard her father had been killed, she grabbed her weapons and armour and rushed off to seek revenge. The Aesir thought it best to placate her, and offered her one of themselves in marriage. But she had to choose by the feet, seeing no more. So the gods held an ankle contest. Skadi saw a very elegant pair of feet, and, guessing it was the beautiful god Baldr, she picked that one. It turned out to be the elderly Niord. As we have seen, their marriage did not take.

Haustlǫng has twelve stanzas on the Thiazi story. Each describes an episode or situation: the first shows Thiazi, in bird's form, watching the Aesir trying to cook their ox, the second reports Thiazi's claim that he prevented the meat being done, the third the gods' offer of some of their meat to Thiazi while Loki worked hard keeping the fire going, the fourth Thiazi's greed in taking such a huge helping, the fifth Loki striking at Thiazi with the staff, and so on. While this is easy enough to follow if you already know the story, it would be tricky – especially considering the contorted language of the verses – to understand the plot if you don't. Again the poem demands audience participation.

Such are the main sources of Norse mythology. There are many others, some minor in the amount of information preserved though they may be major in its importance. To take two examples: as well as the *Prose Edda*, Snorri compiled a Norwegian history called *Heimskringla*, Circle of the World. This comprises biographies of Norwegian kings from the first 'historical' monarch, Harald, nicknamed the Fine-haired, at the end of the ninth century. Before Harald's story there is a book called *Ynglingasaga*, the History of the Kings of the Yngling Dynasty, and here are tales of legendary kings and some of the gods. When Saxo Grammaticus wrote in Latin his history of Denmark, *Gesta Danorum*, early in the thirteenth century, he built upon a lot of mythological and legendary lore, some of it inconsistent with the material we find in, say, Snorri.

From this mixture of sources from different places and times, and responding to different literary demands, it is not likely that we shall gain a coherent account of Norse mythology. There is a confusion of tales: some belong in clear sequences, others are apparently scattered aimlessly about. How much is genuine Norse legend, how much literary invention, is hard to tell. What the myths have to do with Norse belief is also a matter of controversy. A myth, we are told, should employ 'some popular idea concerning natural or historical phenomena'. How far the myths retold here do that is for the reader to decide.☐

Aesir, Vanir and a few kings

I n the Norse myths there are two groups of gods, the *Aesir* (the singular of this noun is *Áss*) and the *Vanir* (singular *Vanr*). Despite Snorri, the word *Áss* is not derived from *Asia*: that is a typical bit of medieval 'learned' etymology. *Áss* derives from a common Germanic word for 'god'. It has a parallel in Old English *ōs* (a word that survives today only as the first element of masculine personal names like *Oswald, Osbert*), and there is a Gothic plural form in a Latin text, *ansis* which is translated *semideos*, 'demi-gods'. *Vanr* is a more problematic word. As the dictionaries admit, 'there is no shortage of etymologies for it', but a tempting one links it with Old Norse *vinr*, 'friend', and Latin *Venus*, 'goddess of physical love'.

The renowned French student of comparative religion, Georges Dumézil, argued that the distinction between the Aesir and the Vanir is an ancient one, to be found in the religions of other Indo-European peoples. The Vanir, he thinks, were originally gods of inferior status, accepted into the superior group only after a period of some conflict. This is certainly reflected in the relationship between the two god types as reported in *Heimskringla*, though there it has become a struggle between neighbouring peoples:

Odin took an army to attack the Vanir. They made a valiant defence of their country, and each side in turn had victory. Each plundered the others' land, doing much damage. And when the two peoples had had enough of this, they set up a peace conference, made a truce, and hostages were exchanged. The Vanir gave their most distinguished men, the rich Niord and his son Freyr. In return the Aesir gave the man called Hoenir, saying he was very proper to have authority. He was a big man, very good-looking. With him the Aesir sent one Mimir, a very shrewd man, and in return the Vanir gave the most intelligent one in their group. He was called Kvasir.

When Hoenir came to Vanaland, he was given authority at once. Mimir taught him everything he should say. And when Hoenir was in attendance at legal moots and gatherings without Mimir at hand, and any difficult case came before him, he always gave the same answer. 'Let someone else decide', he would say. Then the Vanir suspected that the Aesir had tricked them over the hostage agreement. They seized hold of Mimir, cut off his head and sent it to the Aesir. Odin picked it up, smeared it with herbs so that it would not rot, and chanted spells over it. This gave it such power that it spoke to him, telling him many occult secrets.

Odin set up Niord and Freyr as sacrifical priests, and they were cult-leaders among the Aesir. Niord's daughter was Freyia. She was a sacrificial priestess. She was the first to teach the Aesir the practice called *seiðr* [magic] which was common among the Vanir. When Niord lived among the Vanir he had mated with his own sister, for that was legal with them. Their children were Freyr and Freyia. But among the Aesir it was forbidden to mate within this degree of kindred.

Much of this legend is confirmed by allusions in Eddic verses. In the poem *Vafþrúðnismál* the question is asked: 'Where did Niord come from to live among the sons of the Aesir? He controls hundreds of shrines and temples, yet he wasn't born among the Aesir.' The answer is given: 'The wise powers created him in the land of the Vanir, and gave him to the gods as hostage. At the end of the world he will return again to live among the wise Vanir.'

For all the best scandal about the gods, turn to *Lokasenna*, where the insults traded between Loki and his opponents usually reveal some disgraceful act or practice of one or the other. Niord has boasted of his son, loved by all and a prince among gods. Loki retorts:

> 'Stop it, Niord. Control yourself.
> I won't hide this any longer.
> That son of yours you begat on your sister,
> And that's no less than expected.'

When Freyia intervenes, Loki lashes out at her:

> 'Shut up, Freyia. I know you in full.
> You're not exactly free from fault.
> All the Aesir and elves who are in this hall,
> All have been lovers of yours.'

And in his next riposte, he accuses her of being caught in the act with her own brother.

In these verses the distinctive character of the Vanir is affirmed – distinctive but rather sinister, or at least unorthodox. The practice of *seiðr*, for instance, was useful but could be dangerous. It was a form of magic that gave its practitioners power, either to harm others or to achieve esoteric knowledge. Snorri says that Odin knew it, presumably taught by Freyia:

Odin had that skill – indeed he practised it himself – which brought with it great power. It was called *seiðr*. By using it he could learn the fates of men and events still in the future. He could bring death, ill-fortune or sickness to men, or take intellect or strength from one and transfer it to another. But this sorcery, when it was performed, carried with it such effeminacy that it was thought shameful for men to have anything to do with it. So its practice was taught to the priestesses.

In the main, however, the Vanir brought benefits to mankind. Dumézil sees them as 'givers of health, youth, fecundity and happiness'. He speaks of twin deities, and we can think of Freyr and Freyia as twins (as well as mates). Niord too should have a twin sister (and mate), and she can perhaps be traced, though not precisely in Norse myth. Tacitus, the first-century Roman historian, reported a goddess worshipped by Germanic tribes of the North Sea neighbourhood. She was called Nerthus (an exact cognate of the name Niord), which Tacitus glossed as 'mother earth'. She brought peace and fertility to her devotees. Within the Norse sources, Niord is a god of wealth, rich lands, mercantile enterprise and fisheries. Freyr is god of favourable weather and so of produce, of peace and prosperity, and his appropriately virile statue

A phallic figurine from Rällinge, Sweden, perhaps representing the fertility god Freyr.

in the great temple of Uppsala was invoked for fruitful marriages. Freyia 'is very fond of love songs. It is a good thing to pray to her in affairs of the heart.'

Because of the central importance of such themes to daily life in the Middle Ages, there must have been many myths of these Vanir gods, but surprisingly few of them survive. Of some we have hints. For instance, Freyia was married to a little-known god Od, who went off on his travels leaving Freyia weeping. Thereafter she went in search of him, taking upon herself a variety of strange names. There were presumably stories of her adventures, but there survive only a few allusions in Snorri and the poets. When Freyia wept for Od, her tears turned to gold, so a group of kennings for gold includes 'Freyia's weeping', 'the thawing of the eyelid of Freyia', and so on.

Most detailed of our records of the myths of the Vanir is that of Freyr's passion for a giant-girl, Gerd, a love-tale appropriate to a god of fertility and physical desire. It is told in the Eddic poem *Fǫr Skírnis*, Skirnir's Journey, and paraphrased in Snorri's *Edda*. Odin has a great throne, Hlidskialf, from which he can survey all worlds. One day Freyr climbed into it and was punished

29

for his presumption. He looked northwards (and every schoolboy knows that in the north live giants). There he saw the most beautiful girl with shining arms. He fell for her at once and languished, sick for love. Niord, worried at his son's condition, sent for Freyr's squire Skirnir and told him to enquire the reason. Skirnir asked Freyr why he sat moping, appealing to him for the sake of their childhood friendship to reveal his secret. Freyr confessed his love, and begged Skirnir to go a-wooing for him. The journey was likely to be a dangerous one. In recognition of this, Freyr had to give Skirnir his splendid horse and one of his greatest treasures, a sword that would fight of its own accord. Skirnir rode to the giant's dwelling, which was surrounded by howling guard dogs. The shepherd sitting outside advised him against trying to get in. Skirnir persisted. Gerd, following the dictates of northern hospitality, invited him in for a drink of mead, and asked his errand. Skirnir declared Freyr's love, and offered her gifts if she would respond: eleven golden apples and a ring that reproduced itself every ninth night, clear indications of the immense wealth the Vanr had at his disposal. She rejected them; she had enough gold already. So Skirnir resorted to threats, which got more and more outrageous (and to some degree more and more cryptic) until at last she gave in. She arranged a tryst for nine days' time, promising to give herself to Freyr then. Skirnir rode back. Freyr was so eager for news that he was waiting outside. Skirnir gave his message. Freyr's response will smite the heart of all true lovers:

'A night is long. Two are long.
How shall I last out for three?
Often a month has gone quicker for me
Than such a half wedding night.'

For all its obscurities, *Fǫr Skírnis* relates one of the more transparent of Norse myths. The name Gerd has been linked to the common Old Norse noun *garðr*, 'enclosed plot, field' (as in the modern dialectal and specific English word 'garth'), and the coupling of Freyr and Gerd is seen to be an expression of the sacred marriage of the god of fertility to the cultivated land. Ultimately *Fǫr Skírnis* has a happy ending. But it is left to the sardonic Loki to point out the implications in a typical stanza in *Lokasenna*:

'You had Gymir's daughter [Gerd] bought with gold;
That's what you gave your sword for.
But when Muspell's sons ride across Mirkwood,
You wretch, you won't know what to fight with.'

Muspell's sons will be part of the destroying host to attack the gods at the world's end. Freyr will fight to protect the gods, but how can he without the wondrous sword that he gave up in a moment of passion?

Next, a significant tale about Freyr, whose implications are, however, questionable. It comes from Snorri's *Heimskringla*, and so treats Freyr as though he were an early king, not a god; another aspect of that writer's euhemeristic approach to the pagan Norse deities. This affects the story's content. Niord and Freyr are defined as successive kings of the Swedes. Freyr was very popular; in his days harvests were good and there was a long-standing peace, which the Swedes attributed to their king. He established the great temple at Uppsala, applying to it all the money paid in taxes and tribute.

Freyr fell sick, and as the illness gained on him, his men considered what policy to follow. They let few people come near him, and they built a great mound, put a door in it and three windows. When Freyr was dead, they carried his body secretly into the mound, and told the Swedes he was still alive. There they kept him for three years. All the tax money they emptied into the mound, gold in at one window, silver at the second, and the bronze coinage at the third. The period of peace and fertility continued ... When all the Swedes realised that Freyr was dead, yet peace and good harvests still went on, they concluded that so it would be as long as Freyr remained in Sweden, so they refused to cremate him. They called him *veraldargoð*, 'the god of worldly things', and ever afterwards sacrificed to him for peace and good harvests.

Certainly there are some elements in this story – the riches, the fertility – that are characteristic of the god Freyr's adventures, but in fact it is a celebration of kingship as well as godhead. After all, the name *Freyr* was originally a common noun meaning 'lord', related to the Old English word *frea*, used of both earthly and heavenly kings. It seems from the later medieval tales that early Scandinavian kings were revered in proportion to their ability to bring their peoples the blessings of peace and prosperity, to secure productive seasons for crops and cattle. According to some legendary accounts kings who failed in this were killed off. One such wretch, recorded in Snorri's *Heimskringla*, was the fugitive Swedish king Olaf, nicknamed the Tree-trimmer because he fled to the west of the country and vigorously cleared

A reconstruction of the temple at Uppsala, from Olaus Magnus' History of the Northern Peoples published in 1555.

the forests and tilled the land. Other exiles, seeing how fertile the soil was, joined him:

And such a flood of people poured into his territories that the land could not support them all. So there arose great famine and starvation. The Swedes put this at their king's door, because Swedes make a practice of attributing to their king both good seasons and bad. King Olaf was not one for celebrating sacrifices. The Swedes took a poor view of this, thinking it was the cause of the famine. So they gathered together in a band and suddenly fell upon Olaf. They caught him in his house and burnt him in it. Thus they gave him to Odin, sacrificing him to get themselves a good harvest. That was by Lake Vänern.

In his tale of Freyr, Snorri told a royal story which is also a religious one. It resembles an anecdote Saxo Grammaticus tells of the Danish king Frothi, also famed for the long period of peace he brought his people. When Frothi died his retainers wanted to keep it secret so that the land's tranquil condition would remain. They embalmed the body and had it carried round the countryside in a litter, as though the king were too infirm to travel in any other way. Only when the body began to putrefy did they give it proper burial.

This too looks like a transformed religious myth. The name *Frothi* may be related to the adjective *fróðr*, 'fruitful, fertile'. His posthumous progress through the countryside (perhaps to bring an abundant harvest) can be likened to that of Nerthus, *terra mater*, mother earth, in Tacitus's account:

In an island of the ocean is a sacred grove, and in it a consecrated cart covered with a drape. One priest only is allowed to touch it. He becomes aware that the goddess has entered her sacred chariot, and he attends her with great reverence as she is drawn along by her heifers. Then the days are full of rejoicing; the places she thinks worthy of her visit are in festive guise. No-one goes to war. No-one bears arms. All steel is locked away. Only then are peace and tranquillity recognised, only then loved, until the same priest returns the goddess to her temple, having had her fill of human society. Straightaway the cart, the drape, and, if you are prepared to believe it, the goddess herself are washed in a remote lake. Slaves perform this duty, and the same lake immediately engulfs them. From this comes an awesome terror and a feeling of pious ignorance as to what that may be which only those on the verge of death may see.

In turn, the story of a dead king being carried round his realm to ensure that prosperity continued has some little similarity with the tale of the accidental death of the semi-legendary Norwegian king Halfdan the Black, father of Harald the Fine-haired. Snorri tells it in an early section of *Heimskringla*. Halfdan was driving from a feast in Hadeland, and his route took him over the frozen Randsfiord. It was spring and the ice was treacherous. It broke as they were crossing, and Halfdan and all his suite drowned. The bodies were recovered. Halfdan had been a king particularly successful in bringing fertile seasons to his people. The men of Ringerike brought his body home for burial there. To this the people of his other dominions, Rømerike, Vestfold and Heidmark, objected, for they thought that the productive seasons would continue in whatever region the body was entombed. So everybody wanted it. They came to a statesmanlike compromise, chopping the body into four bits and burying a piece in each of the provinces. Hence, claims Snorri, there are four distinct places in Norway called Halfdan's Mound.

The link of the name *Frothi* with the adjective *fróðr*, 'fertile, burgeoning', suggests that it could be a by-name of Freyr. A chapter in the *Ynglingasaga* of Snorri's *Heimskringla* makes it clear that the two names are intimately linked. Snorri takes Freyr to be a Swedish king, successor to Niord in this office. He describes his rule thus:

> He was blessed in friends and fertile seasons as his father had been. Freyr built a great temple at Uppsala, set up his main residence there, and applied to it all his tax-income, his lands and free capital. Then was established the royal treasury of Uppsala, which has continued ever since. In Freyr's days there began 'the peace of Frothi', when there were also fertile seasons in all lands. The Swedes attributed this to Freyr.

Peace and fertility are closely linked in Norse phrase, for it is common to read of sacrifices made *til árs ok friðar*, 'for fruitfulness and peace'. The primitive cult of Nerthus, as we have seen, was also one of peace. Place-names and early references in the sagas confirm this connection between the Vanir and fertile peacefulness. Freyr's name is quite common in Norwegian and Swedish place-names with second elements with meanings like 'meadow', 'field', referring, I suppose, to pieces of land producing rich crops. Niord and Freyr were both wealthy. Indeed, Snorri (or rather High in *Gylfaginning*) says that Niord 'is so rich and blessed with property that he can give wealth of land or of cash to anyone who appeals to him for it'. Freyr owns important treasures like the boar Gullinbursti which lightened darkness with the glitter of its golden bristles. He has a ship with enviable qualities: it can accommodate the whole Aesir band with weapons and armour, it can draw a favourable wind the moment the sail is hoisted, and it can be taken from the sea when not in use and folded up like a cloth and put into a pouch. Freyr's father too had a link with ships and the sea.

For all their differences, the tales of Freyr, Frothi, Halfdan (and in a different mode Nerthus) have common elements, themes that can be supported in different degrees by other early Scandinavian and indeed Germanic stories, that of Olaf Tree-trimmer being only one. The themes are: a deity/king who provides peace and plenty for a people; rich harvests which are connected in popular thought with the continuity of possession of his body, to ensure which abundance the deity/king travels about his realm in a carriage.

Behind legends like these lies some common Scandinavian or probably Germanic myth, and perhaps even some religious ritual derived from it. The Vanir were clearly important deities in the practical concerns of Norse religious activity. They supplied and controlled the wealth on which Norse society, agricultural and mercantile, depended. Not surprisingly, therefore, they are often named as gods to whom sacrifices were dedicated. Paradoxically, it may be this very practical importance that accounts for the comparatively few myths that survive about a major group of gods like this. The twelfth-

The three great gods in the temple at Uppsala. Thor sits in the middle with Odin to his left. Freyr should stand to his right, but the goddess Frigg has been placed there in error. Again from Olaus Magnus' History of the Northern Peoples.

century historian Adam of Bremen compiled a description of the great heathen temple at Uppsala, and the rites conducted there. Within the temple were three major images of gods; one of them, called by Adam *Fricco*, was certainly Freyr, 'doling out peace and delight to mortals'. Adam gives a short account of the great spring sacrifices, but adds disappointingly: 'The chants that are usually sung in the observance of such celebrations are various and unsavoury, so it is best to say nothing about them'.

Inevitably, pagan observances shocked Christian writers and they preferred not to speak of them. If the rites were those of deities who influenced the daily round of life, the economics of agriculture or cattle-raising, the success of trading voyages or fishing, they would be the more dangerous in a proto-Christian society; people would want to carry on with them since the continuity of their communities depended on their success as farmers or seamen. That made it more important for professional Christians to ensure that these gods of the countryside and of the sea were suppressed and their myths forgotten or replaced by Christian equivalents.□

Odin and Thor

The two most famous and powerful of the Aesir, Odin and Thor, stand in sharp contrast to one another: Odin, god of poets and kings, of warriors, of magic; and Thor who appealed to the everyday Viking, the Icelandic or Norwegian man-in-the-fiord. Dumézil viewed the two as types and classified them accordingly. In his division of gods into functions and constituencies, he sees Odin as sovereign god, as king, priest, magician. Thor, he thinks, exhibits the features of the warrior god, one essentially tough and aggressive. There is something in this distinction, though it is simplistic as applied to Viking Age myth or belief. Certainly Thor fights to save the gods from their mortal enemies, the giants; but Odin too has close links with battle, protecting his chosen champions and ultimately gathering them to himself.

Odin

Of the two, Odin was far the more complex in character. This complexity arose, some scholars think, from the circumstance that over the centuries Odin took to himself characteristics and areas of activity that had earlier belonged to other gods. The variety of Odin's nature is mirrored by the large number of names applied to him, names that are not quite nicknames but have something of that quality; what the Norse called *heiti*, a noun related to the verb *heita*, 'to be called'.

Snorri, this time as Third in *Gylfaginning*, says that Odin is the oldest and the most eminent of the gods, in control of all things. The other gods obey him as children do their father – this, of course, was many years ago. Third also calls him *Alfǫðr*, All-father, but he also names him Father of the Slain (*Valfǫðr*), God of the Hanged (*Hangaguð*), God of Captives (*Haptaguð*), God of Cargoes (*Farmaguð*), and, he adds, Odin gave himself even more names on his visit to King Geirrod. Third then quotes a verse list from the poem *Grímnismál*:

'I call myself Grim   Thunn, Unn,
And Ganglari,   Helblindi, Har,
Herian, Hialmberi,   Sann, Svipall,
Thekkr, Thridi,   Sanngetal ...'

And so on for another sixteen lines. No wonder Gangleri bursts out in reply:

'A hell of a lot of names you've given him. My god, what a lot of learning a man must have to be able to tell in detail how each name came into being'.

What in fact a man needs is a grounding in Norse etymology, at any rate for some of the names. *Grímr* is usually interpreted as 'the masked one, the hooded one'. *Herian* is related to the noun *herr*, 'army', and *Hiálmberi* contains the word *hiálmr*, 'helmet'. *Hár* most obviously means 'the high one', but an alternative etymology – suggested but by no means proven – makes it mean 'the blind one'. *Svipall* is linked to the adjective *svipull*, 'changeable, capricious'. In the rest of this verse there are names meaning 'inflamer' (*Hnikarr*), 'weak-eyed' (*Bileygr*), 'fiery-eyed' (*Báleygr*), 'evil-doer' (*Bǫlverkr*), 'long-hood' (*Síðhǫttr*), 'father of victory' (*Sigfǫðr*), 'the blind one' (*Blindi*), 'the one with the magic staff' (*Gǫndlir*), 'gelding' (*Iálkr*), 'feeder' (*Kialarr*), 'destroyer' (*Viðurr*), 'terror' (*Yggr*), 'wind' (*Váfuðr*) and 'god of men' (*Veratýr*). The names show different sides of Odin's character, or something of his variety of action: the god of war and giver of victory, the god of magic, the sinister god, the terrifying and awesome god, the god who could control the winds, the god whose word could not be trusted. Some names enshrine myths. The fact that Odin practised *seiðr*, which could call his masculinity into question, might lead to the name *Iálkr*. The many stories where Odin travels in disguise would account for names like *Grímr* and *Síðhǫttr*. Names like *Bileygr*, *Blindi* and perhaps *Hár* recall that Odin was one-eyed, for he pledged one eye in return for a drink from the well Mimisbrunn, which is the source of wisdom and mother-wit.

Names that evoke warfare and armour suggest the god of battle, the supporter of great fighters, the god who picks for his army the greatest of warriors, men like Eric Bloodaxe. But by virtue of this activity Odin also shows himself faithless, changeable, capricious; after helping a great champion for some time, he will betray him, letting him be killed so that he can come to join Odin in Valholl. Indeed, faithlessness is part of Odin's general nature, as it is part of the way of life of the Vikings, many of whom must have taken Odin as their personal god.

Breach of faith is one of the themes of the Eddic poem *Hávamál*. Therein Odin speaks from his experience of the world, pondering cynically on the treachery men and women show towards one another:

> Loving a woman whose heart is false
> Is like driving an unshod horse over slippery ice,
> A mettled two-year-old, not fully broken;
> Or like handling a rudderless ship in a fierce gale,
> Or like a cripple catching reindeer on the thawing fells.

But in equity he adds:

> Yet now I'll speak plainly. I know both sides.
> Men's minds are treacherous to women.
> When our intent is most false, we speak most fairly;
> That deceives the wisest hearts.

Thereafter he hints at two adventures illustrating these different treacheries. The myths are not told in full, and of the first we have no more information than *Hávamál* supplies. The second can be filled out from other sources.

The first tells of one of Odin's love intrigues that failed. He fell for a girl, apparently a giantess, referred to only as 'Billing's daughter'. He approached her bed, but she begged him to return at nightfall since it would be unseemly for anyone else to know of their mutual passions. Back came Odin at the appointed time, and found all the household guards wide awake, keeping watch with burning torches. He fled, and stole back early next morning. The guards were now asleep, and Odin hoped to slake his desires. But the girl had tied a guard dog to her bed to keep him off.

The second is a story we know already, of Odin's theft of the poetic mead from the giant Suttung. The *Hávamál* poet concentrates on one aspect, Odin's seduction of the giant's daughter Gunnlod in his quest for the drink. By his allusive method the writer requires his audience to fill out the gaps in his tale from their own knowledge:

> The ancient giant I sought out. Now I'm back again.
> Little would I have got by silence there.
> Many words I spoke to my own glory
> In the halls of Suttung.

(Elsewhere *Hávamál* says much about the importance of eloquence to the man who would command success.)

> In a golden chair Gunnlod gave me
> A drink of that precious mead.
> A poor return I made her
> For her true heart,
> For her troubled mind.

There follows an obscure verse, perhaps out of order, that indicates the way Odin penetrated Suttung's rock-girt hall by boring through the crags – or does it tell how he got out again?

> With Rati's mouth I made myself space
> And gnawed through the rock.
> Above and below stood the paths of the giants.
> Thus I risked my neck.

There follows a difficult stanza about the poetic mead, and then:

> I have my doubts if I would ever have escaped
> From the halls of the giants,
> Had I not used that good woman Gunnlod
> Whom I clasped in my arms.

And finally:

> Odin, I think, swore his ring-oath.
> How can his word be trusted?
> He left Suttung swindled of his mead
> And Gunnlod in tears.

We know from elsewhere, including a source from Anglo-Saxon history, that the Vikings held a ring-oath – an oath sworn on a holy ring – in particular reverence. Yet Odin violated his.

There is more than this to the story of Odin stealing the mead, though we cannot always recover it. For instance, part of *Hávamál* is a temperance-tract warning against over-drinking:

> Not so good as people claim
> Is ale for the sons of men.
> The more drink he takes, the less a man
> Knows the thoughts of his mind.

Upon which follow the verses:

> The heron of oblivion it is called
> That hovers over drinking parties.
> It takes a man's mind away.
> With this bird's feathers I was fettered
> In Gunnlod's court.

> Drunk I got,
> Very drunk indeed,
> At the wise Fialar's hall.
> In one thing only is drinking good
> That a man at last recovers his wits.

An intoxicated Odin seducing Gunnlod is a new image. Moreover, if these two verses are linked, Gunnlod's court and Fialar's hall are the same place; Odin stole the mead not from the giant Suttung but from Fialar, one of the dwarfs who made the drink from Kvasir's blood.

Snorri adds a prologue to the story. The dwarfs Fialar and Galar had originally brewed the mead, he says, but Suttung took it over in compensation for the death of his father and mother, a giant Gilling and his wife. The dwarfs had invited Gilling for a row in their boat. It had capsized and Gilling was drowned. Gilling's wife wept copiously, so copiously that Fialar could stand the howling no longer. He encouraged her to seek consolation by going to the doorway and looking out over the place where the tragedy had happened. She agreed. As she stood in the doorway Galar dropped a millstone on her head and killed her. Suttung took exception to all this, and plotted revenge. He grabbed the dwarfs and rowed them out to a skerry that was submerged at high tide. There he threatened to maroon them unless they paid blood-money, and they agreed to give him the mead. He took it home and entrusted it to his daughter Gunnlod.

Odin determined to get hold of the mead. As he walked towards Suttung's stronghold he came to a meadow where nine thralls were mowing. They were the farmhands of Baugi, Suttung's brother. Being thralls they were not very bright, and were using blunt scythes. Odin offered to whet the scythes, and the slaves were agreeably surprised at how much better they then cut. They asked if they could buy Odin's whetstone. He threw it up among them, and they all grabbed for it. What with the confusion and what with the sharp scythes, they managed to cut one another's throats and expired. Odin went on to the farm. Baugi was perturbed that he had lost his entire workforce, but Odin offered to do all their jobs in exchange for one drink of Suttung's mead. He introduced himself as Bolverk, which ought to have put even a giant on his guard, since it means Evil-doer. However, all Baugi did was point out he had no control over Suttung's mead, but he agreed to see what he could do to help Odin with his wish. Bolverk slaved through the summer, and when winter came he asked Baugi for his pay. Baugi went with him to Suttung, but that giant refused to give him a single drop of mead. Baugi and Bolverk plotted to get some nevertheless, and together they drilled a hole through the rock wall to get to the drink. Bolverk turned himself into a snake and wriggled through the hole, and the rest of the story we know.

The tale illustrates several of Odin's unattractive attributes: his low cunning and self-seeking, his ability to change his shape, his propensity for disguises and false names, his recourse to treachery. For a marginally more positive view of the god we should look at his pretensions to being a god of knowledge. Already we have seen ways he achieved wisdom: by sacrificing himself on the tree; by pawning one eye in return for a drink from the well of knowledge. There are others: he could make the dead talk; he could question the wise; he could use the full powers of *seiðr*; he had two ravens, Hugin and Munin, who flew across the word gathering news for him.

Odin's study of cosmology and of past and future events is important to us, for it is enshrined in the small group of wisdom poems which provide much of our knowledge of Norse belief and myth. One of them is *Vafþrúðnismál*, the record of a contest of skill and science between Odin and a giant, Vafthrudnir, renowned for his deep knowledge. The poem opens with a conversation between Odin and his wife Frigg, Odin asking for advice he has no intention of taking. Shall he visit Vafthrudnir to find out how much he knows? Frigg, a dutiful wife, sends him off hoping he will return safely. He reaches Vafthrudnir's hall, addresses him less than tactfully, is nevertheless invited in and interrogated. Typically, Odin gives a false name, Gagnrad. The giant questions Gagnrad briefly, and finding him knowledgeable, suggests a contest: they shall test each other's skills, the loser to forfeit his head. So Gagnrad begins asking Vafthrudnir about the origins of the world, the nature of the gods, the end of all things. The giant replies competently until Gagnrad cheats with his final question: what did Odin whisper into the ear of his son Baldr as the dead god was being put on the funeral pyre? Only Odin knows the answer to this, so the giant realises he has been outwitted:

> No man knows what, in those far-off times,
> You spoke in the ear of your son.
> Doomed I have spoken my old tales
> And told the fate of the gods.
> Now I know it was with Odin I fought,
> Always the wisest of all.

Another wisdom poem with Odin as its protagonist is *Grímnismál*. This is set in a more elaborate narrative frame, given in a prose introduction in the *Codex Regius* text. It tells of two young princes, Agnar aged ten and Geirrod, eight. They went out fishing, and the wind blew them out to sea. They were wrecked on a shore near a small farmer's shack. They stayed with the farmer and his wife that winter, and the farmer took particular notice of Geirrod. When spring came, a ship was found for them. As they were embarking, the farmer gave Geirrod some private instructions. When the ship came to their native land, Geirrod, who was standing in the bows, jumped ashore and pushed the boat back out to sea, leaving his elder brother stranded on it. Geirrod went home, found his father had died in the meantime, was hailed as his successor and grew to be a glorious prince. The rightful heir, Agnar, drifted away in the boat, landed in some desolate place and was taken up by giants living there.

This conflict between two brothers caused strife in higher places, for Odin was Geirrod's patron while Frigg was Agnar's. One day the couple were sitting in their high seat seeing what was happening throughout the world, when Odin observed tactlessly, 'Look at your foster-son Agnar. He's begetting children on a giantess in a cave. Whereas my foster-son Geirrod is a king ruling his country'. Frigg retorted acidly, 'Geirrod is a miser, so stingy with his entertainment that he tortures guests if he thinks too many have come'. This was a slander and they quarrelled over it. Odin bet his wife he could show it to be false.

Odin disguised himself and went to Geirrod's hall to test Frigg's accusation. But Frigg was more cunning than her man. She sent a messenger to Geirrod warning him of this doubtful stranger who had entered his land. Geirrod was taken in, and he made Odin captive. Odin was swathed in a blue-black cloak and gave his name as Grimnir, both of which should have warned Geirrod, had he been bright enough. Geirrod wanted more information. Grimnir stood on his right to remain silent, so Geirrod had him tortured. He built two great fires, set Grimnir between them and left him there for eight days, so scorched that his cloak burned on him. Geirrod had a ten-year-old son whom, with doubtful tact, he had named Agnar after his brother. The young Agnar pitied Grimnir, and brought him a horn full of drink. Grimnir's thanks, and prophecy that Agnar should be rewarded with the throne, opens the verse.

Grimnir then shows the range of his knowledge, naming the courts of the various gods, the supernatural beasts that inhabit their world, telling of the creation of the firmament and the gods' treasures, all things that should waken his audience to his real identity. He ends by foretelling Geirrod's death by the sword, and announcing his name:

> 'Now you can see Odin.
> Approach me if you can.'

The sequel is in prose:

King Geirrod was sitting with his sword half-drawn on his lap. When he heard that his visitor was Odin, he jumped up, wanting to take Odin away from the fire. His sword slipped from his grasp, hilt-down. The king's foot tripped and he fell headlong on to the sword. It skewered him through and he was killed. Then Odin vanished. And Agnar was king there for many years after.

Thor

To turn from the deceitful, sinister and complex Odin to the simple-minded and straightforward Thor is something of a relief. Thor is a battler, his enemies the gods' enemies: giants, monsters and primeval forces. Snorri sums him up:

Thor is the foremost of the gods. He is called Thor-of-the-Aesir or Charioteer-Thor. He is the strongest of all the gods and men ... He has three valuable properties. The first is the hammer Miollnir which the frost-monsters and the cliff-giants recognise the moment it is raised on high (which is not surprising – it has bashed in the skulls of many of their fathers and family). A second splendid thing he owns, his belt of strength; when he buckles it round him his godlike power doubles. A third thing he has which is of the greatest value: his iron gloves. He mustn't be without them when he swings his hammer.

Many myths about Thor survive. Some of them are adduced in early skaldic poems, which shows their great age and perhaps implies a practical worship of the god in Viking times. It may be significant here that Thor is the only god invoked in Viking memorial inscriptions, where such phrases as 'Thor hallow these runes' and 'Thor hallow these monuments' display him as a protecting deity. Yet the myths are not always easy to get at, nor easy to explain in terms other than simple narrative – is there any 'popular idea concerning natural ... phenomena' behind them?

Take the example of Thor's encounter with the giant Geirrod (no relation to the king Geirrod with whom Odin drew conclusions). Towards the end of the heathen age of Scandinavia, the Icelandic poet Eilif Godrunarson wrote a poem which we now know as *þórsdrápa*, the verses about Thor. This survives because it is quoted in Snorri's *Skáldskaparmál*, but it is generally thought of as one of the most dark and difficult of skaldic poems. Snorri gave an interpretation in telling his tale, but who is to say he was right? Snorri's version runs thus.

The trouble began as usual with Loki. One day he was trying out Frigg's falcon-suit in which he could fly around looking like a bird. He came to Geirrod's hall, touched down on the window-sill and looked in. Geirrod did not like this bird watching him, and ordered a servant to catch it. The servant clambered up the wall, and Loki, seeing how severe the climb was, waited till the last minute before flying away, just to annoy the man. Alas, he then found his feet were stuck and he could not escape. Geirrod could see by the falcon's eyes that it was really a man in disguise, and required to know who. When Loki stayed silent, he was shut in a box for three months without food. This friendly persuasion worked, for when Geirrod took him out, Loki was ready to confess. Geirrod offered him his life if he could lure Thor to Geirrod's hall without his mighty hammer and his belt of strength.

What inducement Loki offered Thor for this is not told, but the great god set off unarmed and Loki went along with him. On the way they put up at a giantess's house, and she told Thor the truth about Geirrod's blood-thirsty nature, and lent him a belt of strength, a staff and some iron gloves – you never knew when they might come in handy. When Thor came to the huge river Vimur, he buckled on his belt, took the staff in his hand and waded across, with Loki holding on to the belt. When Thor got midway, the river suddenly rose till it reached his shoulders. He looked about, and there standing in a cleft of the hills and astride the river was Geirrod's daughter Gialp. She it was who had made the water rise. Snorri is too well bred to say how, but presumably she was pissing into the river (which sounds proper for a folk-tale, though some anthropologists and folklorists would prefer her to be menstruating). Thor remarked philosophically, 'Dam a river at its source', and hurled a great rock at her. Then he waded to the bank and heaved himself out by tugging at a rowan. That is why, says Snorri, we call the rowan 'Thor's deliverance'.

This part of the tale is supported by an Eddic stanza that Snorri quotes, perhaps indicating he had a longer poetic version available to him, from which he constructs his prose:

> Rise not, Vimur, since I fain would wade
> Through you to the giants' courts.
> Know if you rise, so will my godlike strength
> Rise up to the high heavens.

Thor continued his way to Geirrod's where he and Loki were shown to a goat-house, hardly fit lodging for deities of their distinction. Inside was a single piece of furniture, a chair. Thor sat on it, and it began to lift under him, pressing him towards the roof. He pushed against the rafters with the giantess's staff to keep himself down, and there was a crack and a scream. Under the seat were Geirrod's daughters trying to crush Thor against the roof. He had broken their backs. Here too there is a verse quotation in Snorri's *Edda*, though it is preserved in only one manuscript:

> One time only I used all my strength
> In the courts of the giants;
> When Gialp and Greip, Geirrod's daughters,
> Tried to lift me to the heavens.

Next Geirrod summoned Thor to his hall which was lit and heated by two great fires. As Thor entered, Geirrod took up a pair of tongs, picked from the fire a red-hot ingot of iron and flung it at the god. Luckily Thor had the iron gloves on. He caught the missile and aimed it back at Geirrod. The giant rushed for protection behind an iron pillar. The ingot crashed through pillar, Geirrod, the wall behind, and into the ground outside. So ends Snorri's story. The final section finds support in a curious passage in

Saxo Grammaticus's *Gesta Danorum*. Recounting an adventurous expedition that the Danes mounted to the north of Scandinavia, Saxo describes some of the terrifying sights they met. They came to a town, an early example of urban decay; within it was a stone hall in sore need of sweeping and garnishing. Therein the Danes saw 'a shattered piece of rock, and not far off on a raised platform an old man, his body pierced, sitting opposite the pile of broken stone'. The Danish leader Thorkell explained to his followers that 'once the god Thor, infuriated by the insolence of the giants, had driven a red-hot steel through the belly of the hostile Geruthus; flying further it had destroyed and thrust through the mountain's sides'. Nearby were the bodies of women, their backs broken.

An odd tale, and one that is as meat and drink to the hungry mythologist. Imaginative interpretations abound. To select a few: is this a myth embodying an initiation test of the manhood of a young warrior; the unarmed Thor facing attack from natural and animal enemies? Does it show divine strength in conflict with the forces of nature; does Thor, here a young and virile god, face the threats posed by 'the dual forces of excessive attachment to the female objects of his primary bonding and the destructive rivalry with the father'? I conclude that of making many interpretations of books there is no end, and much study of them is a weariness of the flesh.

Other stories survive which recount Thor's strife with giants: that of his contest with Hrungnir, for instance. *Lokasenna* treats it as a well-known tale. Towards the end of that poem Loki becomes so outrageous that Thor arrives to quieten him. Loki gives him a sardonic welcome, 'Why are you rampaging about like that?' Thor replies with threats:

> Shut up, you feeble wretch. My mighty hammer,
> Miollnir, will stop your mouth.
> With my right hand I'll smash you with Hrungnir's killer
> So that every bone in your body shatters.

His next verse repeats the offer:

> Hrungnir's killer will send you to Hel,
> Down to the gates of death.

Skaldic poems have other allusions to Thor's destruction of Hrungnir, but again it is Snorri who gives the extended version.

Hrungnir was an ugly giant, with a stone head and a stone heart. His immensely thick shield was of stone, and his weapon was a whetstone, huge enough to be carried on his shoulder. He and Odin quarrelled over the merits of their horses. Odin rode off and Hrungnir followed in fury, galloping so fast that when he came to Asgard he couldn't stop, but crashed through the gates into the court.

The gods courteously invited him in for a drink. Very drunk he got, and began to boast of how he would destroy the gods and kidnap the goddesses. The Aesir sent for Thor who arrived in a great rage, demanding to know who had asked this enemy in and given him liquor. Hrungnir claimed Odin's protection, but agreed to fight Thor on neutral ground, at the border of their territories.

Back went Hrungnir to collect his shield and whetstone. The other giants speculated uneasily on the outcome of the duel, worried that Hrungnir might lose. So they prepared an enormous clay figure of a warrior, with a heart taken from a mare (for only this was big enough, and even this quaked when Thor appeared). Hrungnir stood prepared to receive Thor, with the clay giant, pissing himself with terror, as his second. Thor's second was his servant Thialfi, who was a champion runner and arrived first. He told Hrungnir a disgraceful fib, claiming that the giant should not stand with his shield in front of him since Thor was travelling underground and would get at him from below. So Hrungnir stood on his shield and held his whetstone ready.

Thor arrived in his usual godlike rage and slung his hammer at Hrungnir. Hrungnir retaliated with his whetstone. The two missiles clashed in the middle, the whetstone flew in pieces, part falling to the ground (whence derive all the whetstone rocks of the world). The rest embedded itself in Thor's head and down he fell. Miollnir the hammer followed through and shattered Hrungnir's skull so that he too fell, with his leg upon Thor. Meanwhile Thialfi was butchering the clay giant.

There lay Thor, pinned to the ground by the giant's leg. Nobody could move it until Thor's three-year-old son Magni came and lifted it easily. Thor said politely that he reckoned his son would grow up to be strong.

Thor came home, but the whetstone was wedged in his head. The gods appealed to a witch called Groa, wife of a mysterious Aurvandil. She chanted charms over Thor and the stone fragment loosened. Thor wanted to reward her, so he told her how once he had waded across the chill stream Elivagar, carrying Aurvandil in a basket. One of Aurvandil's toes stuck out of the basket and was frozen. Thor broke it off, threw it into the sky and it became a star. This so delighted Groa that she forgot her charms and the whetstone remained in Thor's head. That is why it is just not done to throw whetstones about in the house; if you do, the fragment quivers in Thor's head. From this myth derive such kennings as 'leaf of Hrungnir's sole' for 'shield', and 'splitter of Hrungnir's skull' for 'Thor'.

Thor is also called 'foe of the World Serpent' in allusion to his struggles with the great monster Iormungand who lurks in the ocean's depths. The tale is illustrated in Viking Age carvings. It is known in some detail from an Eddic poem, *Hymiskviða*. There, however, it forms only one of a series of contests of strength between the terrible giant Hymir and the god Thor, who was visiting him in an effort to seize his great cauldron for the gods to brew beer in. Snorri, who had other source material, relates the story in more telling and elegant terms. He gives no reason for Thor's stay with the giant, merely saying he was on a journey and put up there for the night.

Next morning Hymir was ready to go fishing. Thor wanted to join him but Hymir rejected the offer, saying Thor was too feeble and might get chilled

The Gosforth fishing stone depicting Thor fishing for the World Serpent Iormungand which was so strong that his foot went through the bottom of the boat when he hooked it. The second figure in the boat may be the giant Hymir.

on the open sea. Thor got angry and insisted, so Hymir made him find his own bait. He went to Hymir's herd of oxen, chose the biggest and tore its head off. This he took to the rowing boat that Hymir had launched. The two took up the oars and soon reached the fishing grounds for flat-fish. Thor wanted to go further out and continued rowing. Soon Hymir warned they had better stop, otherwise there was danger of meeting the World Serpent. To Hymir's consternation Thor carried on. At last he took out a great line and a huge hook, put the ox-head on it and threw it overboard. The World Serpent took the bait and the hook lodged in its jaws. The monster jerked back and Thor's hands rapped against the gunwale. At that he lost his temper and heaved so hard on the line that his feet went through the boat's bottom and struck the sea-ground. He hauled the serpent in as far as the gunwale, and there the two glared at one another, the serpent spitting venom. Thor was just going to kill it with his hammer when Hymir, in terror, hacked through Thor's line and the monster escaped. Thor threw his hammer after it, and, says Snorri, or rather High, some say he killed the World Serpent, 'but I disagree; I think it is true to tell you that the World Serpent is still alive, lurking in the encircling ocean'. Thor was so furious with Hymir that he knocked him overboard and himself waded ashore.

The Thor myths I have recounted, though differing widely in detail, have a common theme, Thor's struggle against monstrous beings who can be thought of as enemies of the gods, and presumably also of humans. Extant are other myths of this sort, as well as hints in skaldic kennings of myths that have not survived to us. There are also the stories of how Thor, absent from Asgard, returned just in time to save the gods from trouble, as in the matter of the giant builder who fortified Asgard.

Thor was a specially honoured god in Viking times. In the temple at Uppsala, says Adam of Bremen, there were statues of three gods who can be identified with Thor, Odin and Freyr. Thor, 'the most powerful of them', was placed in the middle: 'he commands the air, he governs thunder and lightning, winds and rainstorms, fair weather and crops'. If disease or famine threaten, Thor is the god sacrificed to. This is not how the Norwegian or Icelandic myths show Thor, but it would account for his popularity in communities built upon agriculture or fisheries. Thor is the only god whose name formed numerous compound personal names in Viking times, both masculine (as *Thorsteinn, Thorfinnr*) and feminine (as *Thorgerðr, Thorgunnr*). The later Icelandic sagas tell of people who venerated Thor as their individual god, as Thorolf from the island of Mostr in western Norway. He 'kept the temple of Thor on the island, was a great friend of Thor, and that is why he was called Thorolf'. In a moment of political crisis he 'held a great sacrificial feast, and consulted his beloved friend Thor as to whether he should come to terms with the king or leave the country and find another way of life for himself; and the consultation directed Thorolf to Iceland'. Nearing that country he threw overboard the wooden posts that had supported the formal seat of honour in his Norwegian ancestral hall. 'Thor was cut on one. Thorolf decided he would settle in Iceland at the place where Thor came to land.' The settlers followed the floating posts and found them driven ashore on a headland in the west of Iceland. 'That,' says the saga, 'has been called Thorsnes ever since.' It still is.□

Baldr and Loki

A famous Norse myth involves two gods quite different in character from those introduced hitherto: Baldr and Loki. Baldr is often named but little known in Norse legend. Snorri says he is Odin's son, the best of gods, fair of complexion and nature, wise, eloquent and full of grace. Yet he is ineffectual. He may be something of a god of law, for his son Forseti controls the great judgment-hall Glitnir where he resolves all disputes. But of the father Snorri admits that no ruling he makes will hold. Baldr must have been something of a fighter too for his name is invoked in kennings for warriors.

Loki has already appeared in this book, and it must be clear that he is a complex figure, part god, part demon. In *Þrymskviða* he was shown to be enterprising, witty, the supporter of Thor while making that great god something of a figure of fun. In the tale of the giant-architect who fortified Asgard, he is shown to be artful, not always wise in his judgment. He brings the gods into trouble through lack of forethought. In the myth of Idunn's apples he betrayed the gods, and only recovered his position with them after threats to his life. At the world's end he is to be one of the leaders of the anarchical army that will destroy the gods; and specifically he is the enemy of the god Heimdall. Snorri sums up the contradictions of his character:

Counted among the Aesir is one whom some call the slanderer of the gods, the father of deceit, the disgrace of all gods and men. He is called Loki or Loptr, son of the giant Farbauti ... Loki is good-looking, pleasing in appearance, but evil by nature and capricious in his habits. Beyond all others he has the sort of mentality that we call cunning, and he devises plots about everything. He has often brought the Aesir into the greatest difficulties, and got them out again by his crafty schemes.

Snorri then lists Loki's illegitimate children by a giantess Angrboda. Her name is a sinister one; it means 'harbinger of grief'. The list of her brood explains this: Fenrir the wolf, Iormungand the World Serpent, and Hel the goddess of the dead. 'And when the gods realised these three siblings were being brought up in Iotunheim, they pursued oracles, and learned that they would bring them immense harm and disaster. All could understand they must expect great evil, first because of the mother's nature, but more so because of the father's.' Odin went to capture the three. He threw Iormungand into the depths of the ocean, and there he remained encircling the inhabited world. Hel he cast into the underworld, to receive all who died of sickness and old age. What happened to Fenrir we have already seen.

The complex figure of Loki has attracted the interest of many scholars, some of whom have even written perceptively about him. Perhaps the most important of recent contributions is that of Georges Dumézil, who sees in the god/demon a reflection of a demonic figure, Syrdon, who appears in a number of Caucasian legends, and argues a common origin for them. If this is true, the concept of Loki as fundamentally at odds with the great gods is an ancient one.

Baldr

It is convenient to begin the myth of Baldr with the relatively late *Baldrs draumar*, Baldr's Dreams, a poem which is not in the *Codex Regius* but in a shorter collection of Eddic material, MS AM 748 4°. This is a question-and-answer poem, beginning as most such do, with a bit of narrative:

> The Aesir came swiftly all to a council,
> The Asyniur [goddesses] too, all in conclave,
> And the mighty powers mulled it over,
> Why Baldr was troubled with dreams of ill omen.

Odin takes action, saddles his horse, rides to the realm of the dead, summons up a dead seeress and asks her to explain. She is reluctant, ending all her pronouncements with the bitter remark, 'Against my will I have spoken. Now I shall keep silent'. Each time Odin is too powerful for her, beginning his questions with:

> Be not silent, witch! I will still question.
> I must know further till I know all.

The re-animated sybil continues helping Odin with his enquiries. Why are there such preparations in the realm of the dead? Answer: they are expecting Baldr to appear; they are brewing mead for him. How will Baldr die? Hod will be his killer, will take the life of Odin's son. Who will avenge this deed?

> In western dwellings Vali will be born of Rind.
> One night old, he will avenge Odin's son.
> He will not wash hands, he will not comb hair,
> Until Baldr's killer is burned on the pyre.

A stanza from *Lokasenna* reveals Loki's responsibility for the crime. Retorting to a threat from Odin's wife, Frigg, he boasts:

> I made sure that never again
> Will you see Baldr riding back home.

Loki has been the *rábani*, 'planner of the killing'; the innocent Hod was the *handbani*, 'hit-man'.

From hints like this Snorri builds up the tale of deceit and evil. It begins with Loki's motiveless malignity, his envy of Baldr. The shining god had had ominous dreams, foreboding death. On behalf of the gods Frigg acted to prevent mishap. She took oaths from all creatures not to harm Baldr: from 'fire and water, iron and all sorts of metal, rocks, earth, trees, diseases, beasts, birds, poison, snakes'. All swore. Baldr became the centre of a game. Since he couldn't be harmed, the gods stood round and used him for target practice, attacking with arrows or spears, swords or axes, stones. Nothing could hurt him. Loki planned disaster. Disguising himself, he went to Frigg and asked why Baldr could not take harm. She told him about the oaths. He asked whether there was anything that had not sworn. Frigg gave the fatal secret away. 'West of Valholl grows a slip of tree called mistletoe. It seemed too young to be asked for an oath.' Loki tore up the tree shoot from the ground, and took it to where the gods were playing. The blind god Hod was standing about doing nothing. 'Why aren't you shooting at Baldr?' 'In the first place I can't see him; in the second, I've nothing to shoot with.' Loki tempted Hod, pointing out what a splendid thing it was to demonstrate Baldr's invulnerability. 'I'll show you where he's standing. Shoot this shaft at him.' Hod shot at Loki's directions, and Baldr fell dead.

Consternation and grief filled the gods. The game had been played at their moot-place, a sacred spot. There they could not take vengeance on Baldr's killer though they knew perfectly well who it was. And they could hardly speak for tears. Frigg showed a woman's practical sense. She sought out someone with the courage to ride to Hel to seek out Baldr and find if he could be allowed to return to Asgard. The great hero Hermod agreed to take this perilous journey, riding Odin's magnificent horse Sleipnir. Meanwhile the gods prepared Baldr's body for the pyre.

This they planned to build in Baldr's ship Hringhorni. It had been drawn ashore, and they could not shift it to the sea. They sent for a witch Hyrokkin, who with a single shove sent it afloat so fast that the runners burst into flames and the whole earth quaked. They carried Baldr's body aboard, and his widow Nanna collapsed with grief and was also put on the pyre. An odd dwarf happened to be passing by, and Thor kicked him on for luck. Treasures were also piled on, including the magical gold ring Draupnir.

Meanwhile Hermod rode the long, dark path to the river Gioll that divides this world from the next. Over its bridge he rode, making it echo as though five legions of the dead were crossing. He came to the gates of Hel, spurred his horse and jumped over. There in the great hall he found Baldr. Hermod asked for his release. Baldr was so much loved, he said. But Hel was sceptical. 'If everything in the world, living and non-living, weeps for him, then he can go back to the Aesir; but he shall be kept in Hel if anything objects or refuses to weep.'

Hermod took back this message. The gods sent ambassadors throughout the world to ask for Baldr to be wept out of Hel, and everything and everyone complied: men, creatures, earth, rocks, trees, all metals. As the messengers were making their way back, they came upon a cave in which sat a giantess named – she said – Thokk. They bade her weep Baldr out of Hel. She retorted with this verse:

> Dry tears are all that Thokk will shed
> At Baldr's funeral pyre.
> Quick or dead, man's son has never served me,
> Let Hel keep her property.

Snorri adds: 'men guess this must have been Loki Laufeyiarson, who has done the greatest wickedness among the Aesir'.

The myth is easily recognised. Though this version has its distinctive Norse features, its type is represented among many mythologies. The myth of the 'dying god', who may also be a resurrected god, is of course central to Christian experience – or at least was before some bishops of the Church of England reformulated its belief. It is also found in, for instance, the Osiris legend of ancient Egypt, that of Adonis from the Near East, and, in heroic rather than mythological form, the Finnish tale of Lemminkainen. Whether there is an archetypal pattern in this or influence of one civilisation's myth upon another is in dispute.

Snorri's story does not end here. Though the gods could not destroy Baldr's killer, they could punish him. Indeed, they became so enraged that Loki fled, taking refuge in a safe house with a door in each wall so that he could keep watch in all directions. By day he became a salmon, living in concealment in a nearby waterfall. When ashore he took the precaution of working out how the Aesir might try to trap him. He thought up the principle of the fishing net, and made up a prototype out of linen thread to see how it would work. Nets have been made that way ever since.

Odin settled into his great throne Hlidskialf. From that eminence he spotted Loki, and directed the gods as to how to find him. When Loki saw them advancing, he threw his net into the fire and fled to the waterfall. The net flared up, but left its pattern clearly to be seen in the ashes. The wise god Kvasir saw it and realised its purpose; so the gods made a similar net and went to the rapids to try to catch Loki. They dragged the river, but twice Loki evaded them, by hugging the shingled bottom or leaping the net. The third time Thor was in wait, and as Loki leapt the net, Thor grabbed him. The gods set to securing him.

They tied him to three great rocks, one beneath his shoulders, one beneath his loins, the third under his knees. In case he was too comfortable, they suspended a venomous snake over him so that its poison dripped on to him. His faithful wife tried to help him by interposing a bowl. However, each time the bowl fills up she has to go off to empty it, and the poison drips on his face. At this he shudders vehemently, and so earthquakes are made. But Loki still lies securely enchained until he is fated to escape and precipitate the final day of this world.

Such is Baldr's story as it is told, hinted at or alluded to in Norwegian/Icelandic writings. Further east, in Denmark, there was a different tradition, one much less picturesque. Saxo Grammaticus recorded it in his *Gesta Danorum*. He thought himself as writing history, not mythology; hence his story is of kings (or at the most of demi-gods and other supernatural creatures),

Figures on the Gosforth Cross (left and above). The lower ones perhaps represent Loki and his wife. Loki is bound and his wife saves him from the poison that drips onto him. This is the gods' vengeance for the death of Baldr.

not of gods. The tale is set in pre-Hamletian Denmark, where Hotherus and Balderus are rivals to the throne, as well as to the favours of the lovely princess Nanna, daughter of Hotherus's foster-father Gevarus. Hotherus was a mere mortal, albeit a talented one, a skilled athlete and musician. Balderus was of more doubtful parentage, being the son of a certain Othinus of Uppsala who, says Saxo scathingly, 'was at that time credited by the whole of Europe with the false title of divinity'. Hence Balderus was a *semideus*, 'half-god'. Hotherus was Nanna's chosen lover, but Balderus fell for her on seeing her bathing, as many a good man before or since.

The stage is set for struggle between Hotherus and Balderus, fighting for the possession of Nanna and control of kingdoms in Sweden and Denmark. Balderus is god-descended, but against this Hotherus has help on several occasions from a group, or possibly groups, of supernatural women (*silvestres virgines, nymphae*, 'wood-nymphs') who control victory and give useful tactical advice. From them he gets a coat of proof which will be helpful in war.

Balderus could not be wounded by steel, so Hotherus needed a special sword to penetrate his thick hide. This he took by force from a supernatural creature, a *satyrus* called Mimingus, who lived in a cave amidst frozen wildernesses. He also seized an arm-ring that had the power of increasing its owner's wealth. Armed with these, Hotherus went adventuring. Meanwhile Balderus accosted Nanna, asked for her in marriage, and got her reply that, being a mortal, it was not seemly for her to mate with a god. This threw Balderus into a love-lorn state.

Hotherus, indignant at Balderus's importunity, gathered a sea-borne army, attacked Balderus and defeated him, even though Balderus had the support of Othinus, Thor and other so-called gods. Balderus fled. Hotherus wedded Nanna. However, this did not finish off his rival. Balderus returned and beat Hotherus in a series of battles. A depressed Hotherus wandered through the forests and again came upon the wood-nymphs. He complained they had not been very successful in giving him victory. They advised him to be philosophical, but suggested more practically that he should steal the supernatural food that gave Balderus his special strength. Curiously encouraged by this, Hotherus again attacked Balderus. After a day of inconclusive fighting with huge loss of life, Hotherus prospected the enemy camp, traced the three nymphs who looked after Balderus's food, tracked them down in disguise and gained (apparently, for there seems to be a loss in the text here) a taste of it. He also got hold of a belt that ensured victory.

Coming back he chanced upon Balderus whom he wounded severely with his magic sword. Bravely Balderus continued the battle the next day from his litter, but his wound was too serious, and he declined and died within three days. Many years later Balderus was avenged when Othinus begat a son, Bous, on Rinda, daughter of the king of Ruthenia. Bous met Hotherus in battle and killed him.

Different as these two versions of the Baldr myth are, they have common details which must come from a common original. Found in both Snorri and Saxo are: the names Baldr/Balderus; Hod (*Hǫðr*)/Hotherus; Nanna; Baldr's immunity from harm save that inflicted by a special weapon; Hod's killing of Baldr; the magical ring Draupnir. From West Norse sources outside Snorri, and also in Saxo, come the name Rind/Rinda as the mother of Baldr's avenger; Baldr as a respected fighter. Yet the variations between the two traditions are immense. Saxo has Nanna married to Hotherus, not Balderus. Balderus is the aggressor, not the kindly and innocent victim. The avenger is called Bous, not Vali (though to confuse the issue, I have to admit that the verse from *Baldrs draumar* that gives this information requires an emendation of the text). But the main difference between the two versions is that in Saxo there is no room for Loki's wicked intervention.

Loki

In the Norse version Loki's part is genuinely devilish. He plays the role of the gods' enemy, motivated only by the desire to destroy. He takes the same part in the battle that ends this world's rule. Naturally there are similarities with the Devil figure in Christian myth, and that may have influenced the late Norse viewpoint. In the tale of the abduction of Idunn, Loki also plays a spoiling game, though there he is forced to it by the straits he finds himself in. At other times his acts are impish rather than devilish. He does trivial works of mischief, which may however have serious consequences.

'Why is gold called "Sif's hair"?', asks Snorri in *Skáldskaparmál*; then he answers his own question. One day Loki cut off all Sif's hair. He did it *til lævísi*, which I would translate 'in sheer vandalism'. Sif's husband Thor lost his temper and was about to beat Loki up, but he hastily promised to go to the elves, very skilled artificers, who would forge a new head of hair for Sif out of gold. This would grow to her scalp like a second crop. So some dwarfs made Loki the hair, and also a ship (Skidbladnir) and a spear (Gungnir). Loki was so impressed that he rashly made a bet – the wager was his own head – with a dwarf called Brokk, who had a craftsman brother, Eitri. The bet was that Eitri couldn't make three things as fine. Eitri set to work, put a pig's skin into the furnace and told Brokk to blow on the bellows and not to stop till Eitri said the word. Brokk started work. As soon as Eitri went off, a fly settled on Brokk's arm and began biting. Brokk ignored it, and when Eitri came back he opened the furnace and took out a boar with bristles of gold which glittered so brightly that they lightened the darkest night. Next Eitri put an ingot of gold into the furnace, and again set Brokk to work with the bellows. Along came the fly again and nibbled at Brokk's neck. Brokk took no notice, and in due course the goldsmith came back and took from the furnace a gold ring called Draupnir. Every ninth night, eight more rings, equal to it in weight, would drip from it. The third time Eitri put iron into the furnace. This time the fly bit at Brokk's eyelids so that blood dripped into his eyes, and for a brief moment Brokk let go the bellows to brush it away. When Eitri came back he said his work was nearly spoiled, but he took from the furnace a hammer. Because of the fly's interference the shaft was just too short. It would never miss its target and would return to the thrower's hand; yet it was so small it would fit inside a man's shirt. Snorri never tells us, but we can be pretty sure the fly was Loki in one of his disguises.

How to decide who had won? Odin, Thor and Freyr were the judges. Loki gave the spear to Odin, the golden hair to Thor, and the ship to Freyr. Then it was Brokk's turn. He gave Odin the ring, Freyr the boar, and Thor the hammer. The gods wanted a weapon to defend them against the giants, so they judged the hammer the best of these treasures. Loki had lost and must forfeit his head. He tried to buy himself out. 'No chance,' said Brokk.

Loki fled, but Thor caught up with him and handed him over. Brokk prepared to cut off Loki's head, but that legalistic god had a flash of inspiration: he could lose his head, but his neck was still his own. So instead Brokk sewed up his mouth, presumably to stop his impish speech in future.

The story has a clear structural purpose within the sequence of Norse myth as Snorri recounts it: to explain how the great treasures of the gods came into being. How far that is an original plan, a real part of Viking Age myth, is unknown. In the tale Loki has no godlike attributes. The most one can say is that he has the supernatural quality of being a shape-shifter, able to take on the attributes of other creatures – but in Norse narrative humans can do this too.

Another of Snorri's tales, that of Thor's expedition to the court of the giant king Utgard-Loki, shows this muted version of the Loki figure. Thor set off on this visit for no defined reason. His companions were Loki and, later, Thialfi. After a surprising adventure with a giant, Skrymir, they reached Utgard-Loki's monstrous palace, where the giant's trickery humbled them. Utgard-Loki challenged them to compete with his own retainers in divers skills. Thialfi chose athletics since he could run faster than anyone. But when matched against the local champion, Hugi, he lost easily. That is because *Hugi* means 'thought', and thought is swifter than anything. Thor competed last, in three contests. He tried to drink off the contents of a horn and failed wretchedly. Afterwards he learned that the other end of the horn was in the sea. His swigging made the tide go out but that was all. The second contest was a silly one: could he pick up Utgard-Loki's rather big cat? He couldn't, but that was because the cat was impersonated by the World Serpent, so long that nobody, even Thor, could raise it. For the third contest Thor suggested a wrestling match, and the giant contemptuously pitted him against an old woman, Elli, who brought Thor down on one knee. That is because *Elli* means 'old age', something that eventually defeats the strongest.

Loki's test, an eating contest, opened the games. Loki bet he could wolf down food faster than anyone else. Utgard-Loki set against him a certain Logi. The two sat at opposite ends of a table, with a wooden trencher full of meat between them. They set off eating as ravenously as they could and met exactly in the middle. Whereas Loki had eaten all the meat off his bones,

Logi had consumed meat, bones, trencher and all. 'And the general opinion was that Loki had lost.' Only later did the gods realise that *Logi* means 'fire', most voracious of all elements.

This side of Loki – a simple figure of fun with no pretence to divinity – must be taken into account, but I suspect his darker, powerful side is more important. Unfortunately, we know too little about the myths that must have circulated about this god, and what we know is varied and sketchy. There survive tantalising references to tales, as that of a struggle between Loki and the strange god Heimdall, a feud to be reawakened at the world's end. On this myth the Icelandic poet Ulf Uggason has an important verse in his poem *Húsdrápa*, composed *c.* 1000. Snorri claims that Ulf wrote a good deal about the story in his poem, but all that remains is the cryptic:

> The gods' famed road-warden, eminent in wisdom,
> Took off for Singastein with Farbauti's crafty son.
> Son of eight mothers and one, powerful in mind,
> He first took possession of the brilliant *hafnýra*.

Again the audience has to spot the references. Heimdall was the guardian of the paths of the gods: he it is who, on the final day, will blow his horn to signal the approach of hostile forces. He was also that obstetric curiosity, born to nine mothers. Farbauti's son was Loki. So somehow Loki and Heimdall went to Singastein where Heimdall got hold of a *hafnýra*, a curious word that occurs only in this verse. Literally it means 'sea-kidney', and anyone may have a guess at what that might be. Snorri came up with an answer in his *Skáldskaparmál*. 'Heimdall is the visitor to ... Singastein. That was when he fought with Loki for the *Brísingamen* ... They were in the guise of seals.' Apparently Singastein was a rock in the ocean, hence the gods' peculiar disguises. The *Brísingamen* is well known (though what it has to do with 'sea-kidneys' I haven't the least idea). It was a famous and glorious gold necklace, some time the property of Freyia. According to a late text, it was made by four dwarfs, and the goddess so coveted it that she slept with each dwarf in turn and got the necklace as payment. Which sounds typical of her. More than this we do not know, save that at the world's end Loki was to seek out Heimdall and fight him to the death.□

Beginnings, middles and ends

Most – perhaps all – peoples ponder on the distant past and the distant future: how did this world begin and what was there before; what are the limits of the world and how are they set; how was man created (seldom why); how will the world come to its end, and then what will happen? Such ponderings are a potent source of myth, specifically here of Norse myth. The answers the Norsemen gave these questions are unlikely to be coherent and are certainly not comprehensive. Nor need we assume there was a single, orthodox belief to be expressed.

A good place to begin is with the early part of the great Eddic poem *Vǫluspá*, The Wise Woman's Prophecy. This probably dates from *c.*1000, when Christ was beginning to exercise a strong influence on Norse affairs. So the poem as we have it may show Norse myth infiltrated by Judaeo-Christian. Moreover, the *Codex Regius* text of this poem shows it already in mutilated state; there are obvious gaps in it and there are likely to be inter-polations that are harder to trace. Even our primary source is thus defective. The poem is presented as the pronouncement of an unspecified *vǫlva*, 'prophet-ess, sybil', at the insistence of Valfodr, one of Odin's many names. He had asked her to relate 'the ancient tales of men', the first things she could remem-ber. From her memories of primeval times, she went on to speak of later, though still ancient, events, and finally to the future which she foretold, pre-sumably to Odin's apprehension. Of the earliest state of the universe she says:

> It was in distant times
> When nothing was;
> Neither sand nor sea
> Nor chill waves;
> No earth at all
> Nor the high heavens;
> The great void only
> And growth nowhere.

So far so clear. But then the story becomes so allusive as to be cryptic. Bur's sons, she says, raised up lands and shaped Midgard, the central enclosed territory of inhabited earth. Greenery spread over it, but the heavens were not yet planned. The sun, moon and stars did not know their functions and places. So the gods – the word here is *regin* which means something like 'organising powers' – sat in conclave, discussed the situation, and determined the hours of day and night and the division of time into years. They met together on a plain called Idavoll, perhaps meaning Evergreen Field. There they built houses and temples, set up forges, made tools and worked precious metals. So they lived in bliss, wealthy beyond need, and playing some sort of board game with golden pieces by which, think some, they determined the world's course. Then disaster struck. The problem is we do not know what it was. It was connected somehow with the arrival of three monstrous giant women, but at this stanza any continuity the poem had is broken. Snorri Sturluson himself did not know the answer.

Even an amateur cosmographer can pick plenty of black holes in the *Voluspá* story. There are too many things unexplained. Who were Bur's sons (Odin and his two brothers?) and where did they spring from? Who made the heavenly bodies? What was the origin of the gods, and how did they achieve their 'organising power'? And so on. This lack of information in *Voluspá* may, of course, be the effect of that poem's defective transmission and record. Snorri obviously found difficulties, but he made a rather better effort at explaining the creation, largely by interpreting the additional material found in the question-and-answer poem *Vafþrúðnismál*. When Gangleri/Gylfi questioned the three mysterious kings, one of his first enquiries was, 'What was the beginning? How did everything begin? What was there before?' High replied by reciting the *Voluspá* verse I have quoted (and indeed, reciting a better form of it than appears in *Codex Regius*). But the kings obviously thought this was inadequate, for they went on to add to the account, though it is not always easy to see what they meant. They define a universe, part freezing (called Niflheim, Land of Fog), part hot and blazing (called Muspell). These two regions stand on either side of the Great Void (Ginnungagap). A river flowed into Ginnungagap, and froze over, layer upon layer, forming a fundament. Where hot and cold met, the rime began to melt, and its drops, quickened by the warmth, formed a frost-giant, Ymir. From him, by a remarkable feat of parthenogenesis, the race of frost-giants descended: 'beneath his left arm grew a man and a woman, and one of his feet begot a son on the other.'

Gangleri tried to understand the logistics of the situation: what did Ymir live on? 'The next thing that happened, as the rime continued dripping, was that it formed a cow called Audhumla. Four rivers of milk flowed from its teats, and it fed Ymir.' But what did the cow live on? 'It licked the rime-stones since they were salty. The first day it had been licking the stones, in the evening there appeared from the stones a man's hair, the second day a man's head, and the third the whole man. He was called Buri.' Buri mated (but Gangleri forgot to ask with whom) and begot a son called Bor who married a giantess by whom he had three sons, Odin, Vili and Ve.

There were giants in the earth in those days, and the same thing happened to them as happened to those of Noah's time. Odin, Vili and Ve slew Ymir, and so much blood poured from his wounds as to drown nearly all his progeny. One called Bergelmir escaped with his family by jumping into his *lúðr*, a word that seems to mean 'chest, coffin', but which Snorri apparently equated with 'ark'. Ymir's corpse was not wasted. Odin and his brothers carried it to Ginnungagap, and set it in the midst. His flesh was made into the earth, his bones into crags; his teeth and bits of his shattered bones became shingle and small rocks. His blood was standing water and sea, encompassing the earth on all sides. More elegantly, the brothers created the sky out of Ymir's skull, and under each cardinal point of the compass they put a dwarf (where did they come from, I wonder?), presumably to hold it up. Odd sparks and molten particles that shot up out of Muspell they caught and set in the heavens, some fixed to the sky and others moving freely beneath it. The brothers had still not finished recycling Ymir. They took his brows and made them into a protecting wall to keep men safe from the giants; within this wall was Midgard, the central enclosure where humans dwelt. Ymir's brains they threw into the sky to form clouds. High justifies this story by citing stanzas from another question-and-answer poem, *Grímnismál*:

> From Ymir's flesh was the world fashioned,
> And from his blood the sea.
> Crags from his bones, trees from his hair,
> And the vault of heaven from his skull.

> And from his brows the genial gods
> Made Midgard for mankind.
> And from his brains were all those
> Harsh storm-clouds created.

Within this world were to dwell a variety of beings, men, gods, monsters, giants and elves. The geographical relationship of their different dwelling-places to each other is unclear, and probably always was. Snorri made a stab at defining it. The giants, he said, live by the deep ocean, at the outer edge of the circular world. Men reside nearer the centre, in their protected land called Midgard. Elves are of two sorts: swarthy ones who lurk within the earth, and brilliant ones who live in Alfheim. The gods and goddesses make their home in Asgard, each within his or her own sanctuary. At the most sacred place of all, at the earth's centre, the gods hold their daily courts, under the great ash-tree Yggdrasil, whose boughs spread over the whole world. Beneath one of its roots is Mimir's well, wherein is hidden all wisdom and good sense. When Odin wanted to gain wisdom by taking a single drink from this well, he was required to leave behind one of his eyes as a pledge. Hence Odin is always portrayed as one-eyed. There is a second spring beneath the tree's roots, called the Well of Fate. By this is a great hall in which live three demi-goddesses called Urd, Verdandi and Skuld (meaning something like Fated, Happening, What Must Be). These are the Norns who shape the course of men's lives. At this point Snorri suggests there is a confusion in Norse myth, for he also mentions individual norns, attached to a man at his birth and controlling his destiny, not always for the happiest. As Gangleri comments: 'If norns control men's destinies, they arrange things jolly unfairly; some people have a good and splendid life, some have not much success or glory; some have long life, some a short one'. And to this eternal problem

High has no very convincing solution.

There is nothing eternal about the state of this world. Even the great world-ash is subject to attack. Snorri quotes a verse from *Grímnismál* about the tree's enemies:

> The ash Yggdrasil endures hardship
> More than men can know.
> The hart bites its crown, its sides decay,
> The serpent Nidhogg tears its roots.

The Norns try to preserve it by pouring over its branches water and mud from the Well of Fate. This magical liquid helps to stop the rot. In the end the tree is to fall, as are the gods themselves. They are as mortal as man.

Another myth tells the beginnings of mankind. The primary source is a couple of stanzas in *Vǫluspá*. The text of the poem is in disarray here, nor can we be sure if these verses are original or late interpolations. Certainly the details of the story are confused, and its beginning (its end too) is abrupt:

> Until from that band there came three
> Mighty, great-hearted Aesir to that dwelling.
> By the shore they found two of little strength,
> Ask and Embla, beings without destiny.
>
> No breath they had, no living soul,
> No flow of blood, no voice, no colour.
> Odin gave breath, Hoenir gave soul,
> Lodur gave both blood and colour.

Snorri had to make sense of these stanzas for his *Prose Edda*. He succeeded, but by adding and altering. He makes Gylfi ask where the people who inhabit the world come from. High answers:

Bor's sons [Odin, Vili and Ve, an alteration from the *Vǫluspá* version here] were walking by the sea-shore, and came upon two logs. They picked them up and shaped them into human beings. The first gave them breath and life, the second understanding and motion, the third form, speech, hearing and sight. They gave them clothes and names. The man was called Ask [ash tree], the woman Embla [perhaps 'elm' or 'vine']. From them descend the races of men who have been given a dwelling-place below Midgard.

For the beginnings of social class in this world, we turn to another, rather unusual, poem called *Rígsþula* or sometimes *Rígsmál*, the Tale of Rig. Though it is an Eddic poem it does not appear in the *Codex Regius*. Its primary text is in a manuscript of Snorri's *Prose Edda*. The story tells of Heimdall, a rather shadowy god, indeed so shadowy it is not always clear if he is *Áss* or *Vanr*. He went on his travels, taking the name of Rig which has been linked to an Old Irish word *ríg*, 'king', since the poem tells of the origin of royal and other ranks. Thus there is a suspicion of Celtic influence on the myth. The poem's prose introduction runs:

In ancient histories men say that one of the Aesir, the one called Heimdall, was off on his travels. He walked out to the sea-shore, came upon a farmstead, and gave his name as Rig. This poem follows that history.

The god is defined as *kunnigr, rammr* and *rǫskr*, knowing, tough and vigorous, suitable qualities for the work he will do in the poem. In the farm kitchen sat two aged people, Ai and Edda (Great-grandpa and Great-grandma). They welcomed Rig and dined him as best they could on coarse bread and broth. Then they all went to bed, Rig lying between the couple. In nine months Edda gave birth to a boy-child. They called him Thrall. He grew up to be strong, but rough and ugly, capable of hard, menial toil. He married a suitable mate and they raised a family, all with vulgar names. These would do the heavy work on the farm: muck-spreading, tending the beasts, peat-digging. So arose the race of slaves.

Rig walked on and came to a more prosperous-looking house. Inside sat a well-dressed couple. The man was a skilled workman and farmer, the woman was spinning. They were called Afi and Amma, Grandpa and Grandma. They welcomed Rig and presumably (there seems to be a lacuna in the poem here) gave him a rather better supper than his former hosts. They went to bed, Rig again between the pair. Nine months later Amma bore a boy-child, ruddy-faced and with peering eyes. They called him Karl. He grew up to be a craftsman, skilful worker and farmer. His bride was keeper of the household, looking after the linen, holding the keys to the locked chests. Their family formed the race of yeoman farmers.

On walked Rig and came to a splendid mansion, occupied by another couple, Fadir and Modir, Father and Mother. Fadir was checking his armoury, making sure his bow and arrows were in good order. Modir seems to have been occupied with her appearance; certainly she was very fashionably dressed. She took her best linen cloth and set out a sumptuous supper on a silver service, fine bread, pork and roast fowl, with wine to drink. They sat and chatted; then to bed as before. Nine months later Modir bore a boy-child, fair-haired, clear of complexion and with eyes as keen as serpents. He was called Earl. He grew up to be the aristocratic sportsman and fighter, learning to shoot, wield a spear, fence, ride and swim. This son Rig acknowledged, taking an interest in his education, teaching him about runes, granting him estates. The lad grew into a great and wealthy warrior, a generous prince. He married and had aristocratic children. The youngest was called Konr, and here the poet indulges in a pun: *Konr ungr*, 'the young Konr' becomes *konungr*, 'king'. And at that the poem breaks off.

The myth is transparent. All human beings derive ultimately from the gods, but they are not equal. Indeed, the poem *Vǫluspá* opens with a call for silence from all Heimdall's kin, great and small. The greatness or smallness of a man's social position depended on family. This applied in particular to kingship, for the meaning of the word 'king', *konungr* in Old Norse, *cyning* in Old English, is 'man of kin'. A man or woman's skills, appearance, rights and duties derived from the social position (s)he was born to. Norse life was aristocratic, fixed in social dimension, its ranks set firmly.

For mankind death is a necessary end, we are told, which will come when it will come. Yet many peoples have been reluctant to see death as an end, preferring to think it a transition to another life; and they have evolved myths to expound this. Norsemen were no more willing than most to meet their end, and they have many tales that tell of life after death: a shadowy life in a grave-mound; a life that allows the dead to walk again; a life of revelry within a holy mountain; and so on. These, though delightfully improbable, are hardly mythology. Their variety suggests there was no very clear-cut or coherent view of the dead that applied to the whole of pagan Scandinavia. Mythological stories and references confirm this variety of attitudes, giving inconsistent accounts, some of them very slight indeed. For instance, Snorri's *Prose Edda* lists, among the goddesses, a little-known one called Gefion: 'she is a virgin, and those girls who die as virgins are her servants'.

A stanza from the Eddic poem *Hárbarðslióð* also tells of a division of responsibility for or claim on the dead:

> Odin owns the fighting-men who die in battle,
> And Thor takes the race of slaves.

An alternative disposition is recorded in *Grímnismál*:

> That place is called Folkvang where Freyia disposes
> Of seating-places in her hall.
> Each day she picks out half the slain,
> The other half has Odin.

To the outgoing warriors of Viking times, the myth with the greatest appeal was that of Odin taking to himself those who died in war. Freyia's share is usually not mentioned, though Odin is certainly seen to be exercising discrimination, picking out the ones who show themselves most valiant. His assistants are demi-goddesses, valkyries; indeed the word *valkyria* (*valr*, 'those slain in fight'; -*kyria*, connected with the verb *kiósa*, 'choose') means 'one who picks from among the war-dead'. When King Hakon the Good of Norway died of wounds received in battle *c.* 960, his court poet, Eyvind (nicknamed 'despoiler of poets' because he stole other skalds' ideas), composed a funeral ode for him. Though Hakon had been a Christian – hence his sobriquet – Eyvind modelled his dirge on *Eiríksmál*, the pagan poem written for Eric Bloodaxe. It begins with two valkyries, Gondul and Skogul, being briefed for a mission:

> Gautatyr [Odin] sent Gondul and Skogul
> To choose among the kings;
> Which one of Yngvi's race should go to Odin
> And dwell in Valholl.

> They came upon Biorn's brother [Hakon], clad in mail-coat,
> A glorious king beneath his battle-banner.
> Lances levelled, pennant fluttered,
> As the clash of war began.

Hakon is a star performer:

> So the sword in the prince's hand
> Bit Odin's gear [armour] as though plunged into water.

Spear-points clattered, shields smashed,
Swords hammered into men's skulls.

The valkyries, recognising the talent, choose Hakon to join Odin's forces. Hakon is not impressed; he sees no future in dying in battle:

'Why did you thus dispose the fight, Gondul?
Did we deserve no success from the gods?'

The retort is:

'It was we who allowed you to hold the field,
And made your enemies flee.'

Hakon is still not satisfied, particularly since he distrusts Odin who is notoriously *illúðigr*, 'black-hearted'. Though the valkyries promise him safe conduct to Odin's hall, and plenty to drink when he gets there, he insists on holding on to his arms and armour:

'Always guard helmet and mail-coat well.
It's good to have them at hand.'

The gods welcome Hakon to their land, but the poem concludes with an ominous verse looking to Odin's need for such men in his army.

Unchained, wolf Fenrir will invade men's homes
Before so good a king returns to these desolate tracks.

Life in Odin's hall, Valholl, is good if you like that sort of thing. *Grímnismál* tells quite a lot about it, and Snorri takes up this information into his *Edda*, expanding and rationalising it, and commenting quizzically. Since the battle-dead of centuries have been collected into Valholl – and Snorri implies all of them, not part only – it has to be an enormous building:

Five hundred doors and forty more
In Valholl I think there are.
Eight hundred warriors at a time
Will pass each door to fight the wolf.

Even then, says Snorri balefully, and even with all those to be added from future wars, they will not seem too many when Fenrir attacks. The commissariat for this mighty army is the cook Andhrimnir, who has a great cauldron Eldhrimnir. Into this every day the cook puts the meat of the great boar-pig Saehrimnir, to make pork stew for the fighters. Each night the pig is whole again. The drink is mead, also produced by an unconventional process. A goat Heidrun lives on the roof of Valholl, feeding on the foliage of a tree called Lerad; from the goat's teats flows so much mead that she fills a great barrel every day. 'That', says Gangleri wonderingly – or perhaps ironically – 'is a jolly convenient goat to have. And it must be an extraordinary tree it feeds on.'

Odin himself is more abstemious. As he presides over the feasting he takes only wine, which serves as food and drink for him. Meat put before him he feeds to his pet wolves Geri and Freki.

There is a further shadowy place mentioned in the literature as the abode of the dead. It is called Hel, governed by a goddess of the same name: a wretched place divided from the world of men by the river Gioll, over which arches the bridge called Giallarbru. It was this way that Hermod rode when he visited the realm of the dead to seek out Baldr. Snorri describes precisely how to get to Hel: *niðr ok norðr liggr Helvegr*, 'the road to Hel runs downwards and northwards'.

From time to time but insistently in this book, and throughout the Eddic and skaldic literatures too, there has been mention of the end of the world, the great calamity that Odin tries to evade by assembling his army of chosen and veteran warriors. This is *Ragnarǫk*. The word is a compound. Its first element, *ragna-*, is the possessive plural of the word *reginn* which we have seen used of the gods as organising powers. The second part, *-rǫk*, means literally 'marvels, fate, doom'. Thus the compound literally means 'fate/wonders of the gods', but quite early the second element became confused with the word *rǫkkr*, 'twilight'; hence Wagner's *Götterdämmerung*, 'twilight of the gods'.

The gods know that Ragnarok is inevitable. It has been prophesied that they will be destroyed in this final battle, yet they prepare for it. Their greatness is shown in their defiance in face of a fate that they cannot avoid. Again, *Vǫluspá* is our primary source for the detail of this struggle, though numbers of other poems allude to it. Snorri took over the *Vǫluspá* account, quoting freely from it as well as interpreting it liberally. The final age of this world is to open with terrifying omens. There will be a fierce winter, *fimbulvetr*, 'the monstrous winter'; 'those winters go three in a row with no summer in between'. Strife will fill the world, even strife within families which cuts at the heart of Norse social thinking. Ethical bonds will dissolve. There will succeed:

> An age of axes, an age of swords, shattered shields,
> An age of tempests, an age of wolves, before the age of men crashes down.

Here there is an echo of the terrors that presage the coming of Antichrist in Judaeo-Christian mythology, and we should keep in mind that *Vǫluspá* probably dates from a time when Norse paganism was giving way before Christianity.

There are natural portents. High had explained to Gangleri that the sun and moon race across the heavens pursued by wolves trying to eat them. At Ragnarok, we now learn, the wolves will catch up.

One wolf will gulp down the sun, and men will think that a great disaster. The other wolf will catch the moon, and he will not produce much improvement either. The stars will fall from the sky. And this too will happen; all the earth and the mountains will quake so that the woods are loosened up from the ground, and the crags totter, and all fetters and bonds will shatter and tear apart. And then the wolf Fenrir will get free.

The attack on the gods is confusedly told in the poetic sources and in Snorri's prose version. It needs a good deal of rationalisation to get a coherent

A monster swallowing a male figure (above) which may of course be interpreted as Odin meeting his fate at Ragnarok. From the church of Torpo, Hallingdal, Norway.

A man fighting a monster on the Gosforth Cross – Odin at Ragnarok again?

story, and what follows here is only one such. There are three main invading forces. From the sea slithers the great World Serpent Iormungand, in fighting mood. It creates tidal waves which loosen the ship Naglfar (a name which Snorri interprets as 'nail-ship', made from the uncut nails of the dead, an excellent reason why anyone should keep his nails well-manicured). In this ship is the giant Hrym, and apparently the sons of Muspell too, whoever they may be. Loki, also freed from his bonds, is the helmsman. From the south advances the fire-demon Surt with his army (which some think includes Muspell's sons). Most fearsome of all, the ravening Fenrir races forward, his jaws agape so that, says Snorri, the upper one touches the heavens, the lower the earth. 'He would open them wider if only there were space.'

Heimdall blows his horn to summon the gods to war council. Odin consults Mimir's head but it is too late. The gods arm. Freyr fights Surt, but he is inadequately armed – he has given his splendid sword to Skirnir – and so he is cut down. Thor manages to destroy Iormungand, but is overcome by its venom and falls dead. Fenrir gulps Odin down. Odin's son, Vidar, avenges his father either, according to *Vǫluspá*, by stabbing Fenrir to the heart, or, according to Snorri and *Vafþrúðnismál*, by stepping with a heavily-shod foot on its lower jaw, pulling upwards on its upper jaw, and tearing it in two. (Where did he find space for that, I wonder.) Snorri adds two more duels, neither, I think, otherwise supported. Garm, a monstrous hound, and Tyr kill each other, as do the traditional enemies Loki and Heimdall. Thereupon Surt scatters fire over the whole earth, and it burns away.

The tale is nicely schematised, but it is hardly satisfactory. It tells so little. There is no general scheme of battle between the forces of the gods and those of darkness. What about the other gods whose names we know? What happens to the goddesses? Where are Odin's chosen warriors, who have trained so hard for this fixture?

Nevertheless, Ragnarok means the end of the old gods' regime. Yet though I have elsewhere translated the phrase 'the end of the world', it is in fact not the close of everything. *Vǫluspá*, and Snorri following it, tell of a new beginning, perhaps intended as heralding a new world purged of the treachery of the old one, or at least punishing such wickedness. Obviously there is likelihood of Christian influence upon Norse myth here. Gangleri asks the significant question:

What happens after heaven, earth and the whole world is burnt up, and the gods are all dead, and all the great warriors, and all humankind? Didn't you tell me that every human being must live throughout all time in some world or another?

Third gives the grim answer, 'There will be many good forms of life and many bad', and then provides examples of each. If you have been virtuous you may live on in delightful surroundings, which could mean enjoying drink-ing in the hall called Brimir, or having, I suppose, a life of ease in the golden hall Sindri. In contrast – and here Snorri quotes from *Vǫluspá* – there is another hall in a place with the unpromising name *Nástrǫnd*, 'corpse-beaches'.

Its doors face northwards, not a good sign. It is built of interwoven serpents, whose poison floods the building. Those who lodge here are the oath-breakers and brutal murderers.

But there is another renewal. The visionary of *Voluspá* puts it thus:

> A second earth she sees arise
> From out of the sea, green once more,
> The cataracts tumble, the eagle flies over them,
> Hunting fish in the mountain streams.

> The Aesir meet again on Idavoll
> And speak of the mighty World Serpent,
> And call to mind the mighty judgments
> And the ancient mysteries of the Great God himself.

There is even a reference to that strange board game that was a feature of the early (and innocent?) life of the old gods:

> Then again will be found in the grass
> Those wondrous golden playing-pieces,
> Those they had owned in ancient times.

Whether in consequence, or simply afterwards, a golden age will come. Fields will flourish unsown – one of man's perpetual dreams – and all ills will be cured. Baldr will return, and the children of the old gods will take over their heritage. According to Snorri (not in *Voluspá* but in *Vafþrúðnismál*), two humans will survive the holocaust, nourished by the morning dews. From them the new race of men will be born.

So the whole sad business starts again. Gangleri would doubtless have wanted to know more, but High shuts him up firmly. 'If you want to know anything after this, I've no idea where you are going to learn it from. I've heard nobody tell the future of the world beyond this point. So make the most of what you have learnt.' Which is probably as far as any philosopher has got.☐

Gods and Heroes

S
o far the myths of gods and goddesses have shown them in some isolation from mankind. They have told of actions that affect deities only (as in the Baldr myth), or of often stormy relationships between gods and other supernatural creatures – giants, demons, dwarfs and so on (as in the story of Idunn's kidnapping). Odin had an interest in the warrior class, helping professional fighters before betraying them. Inevitably the gods are linked to humanity in the cosmic creation and destruction tales. But otherwise, in the myths included here, there has been little connection so far between god and man.

However, there is one powerful myth – powerful in its enduring effect on European culture – that illustrates the way an action of the Aesir could affect the fates of individual humans, a myth that connects an adventure of the gods with a cycle of legends of heroic kings and fighting men. This turns on a question asked in my first chapter and not yet answered: why is gold referred to as 'the otter's blood-money'? The story is told in one of the Eddic poems, *Reginsmál*, the Tale of Regin, together with its prose intro-duction in the *Codex Regius*. Snorri has a version in the *Prose Edda*, and it also occurs, essentially linked to heroic actions, in a late medieval Icelandic saga called *Vǫlsunga saga*, the History of the Volsungs, about which more later.

The tale begins with a rich farmer called Hreidmar. He had magical skills, and not surprisingly all his three sons had peculiar characteristics. Two of them were shape-changers, Fafnir and Otr. The third was a dwarf, Regin. Like all dwarfs he was a fine craftsman, in particular a smith. He was also, says the *Codex Regius* ominously, 'knowledgeable, savage and skilled in magic'. Otr had the curious practice of turning into an otter (which is what his name means) and living in a torrential river, eating the fish he caught. This was his undoing.

One day a trio of gods, Odin, Hoenir and Loki, were out on one of their expeditions, and as usual Loki got them into trouble. This time by an incautious though excusable act. They came to a waterfall, and on the river-bank nearby spotted an otter devouring a salmon. Like all otters, says *Vǫlsunga saga* (and it would be interesting to know if this is a fact of natural history), this otter was eating with its eyes shut. The saga's explanation is that the otter couldn't bear to see his meal getting less the more he ate of it. In any case, the otter did not see the gods approaching. Loki threw a stone at it, killed it, and so in one blow gained both an otter skin and a salmon. The gods thought this a lucky strike until they came to Hreidmar's house and asked for a night's lodging. They boasted of their catch and showed Hreidmar the otter skin. The farmer and his sons recognised it, grabbed hold of the three gods and demanded compensation. The Aesir agreed to fill the skin with gold and then pile gold all over it until it was completely covered. Loki was sent off to find the wherewithal.

Luckily he knew of a dwarf called Andvari; dwarfs, being skilled craftsmen, usually had plenty of gold about them. This dwarf again was an odd character. He assumed the form of a pike, and lived in a waterfall catching fish. Loki borrowed a net from the sea-goddess Ran and caught the pike. *Reginsmál* records the conversation between them. Loki asked:

'What sort of fish is this, swimming in the flood,
Yet it cannot save itself from disaster?
Ransom your life from the realm of death
And get me gleaming gold.'

'Andvari's my name, Oin my father's,
Through many a torrent I've swum.
In ancient times a cheerless fate
Decreed I should wade in water.'

As ransom Loki demanded all Andvari's gold. The dwarf paid up, but tried to hold back a single ring (presumably an arm- not a finger-ring) since this had magical properties that would help him recoup his fortunes. Loki exacted the ring from Andvari. Leaving for the security of his home in a rock, the dwarf cursed whoever held his treasure:

'That gold [the word could also mean 'ring'] that Gust once owned
Shall be the death of two brothers,
Shall be the downfall of eight princes.
In my wealth shall no man delight.'

Loki brought back his plunder, and Odin, coveting the ring, kept it for himself. The rest of the treasure the Aesir used in stuffing the otter skin and covering it with gold. Hreidmar inspected their effort, and spotted a single otter hair uncovered. Reluctantly Odin pulled off the ring and covered the hair. As the gods departed from Hreidmar's hall Loki revealed the dwarf's curse:

'To you now gold, great ransom
Is rendered for my life.
For your son no fortune will follow.
This will bring death to both.'

So it did. Fafnir and Regin asked for their share of the blood-money, but Hreidmar would not pay up. Fafnir killed his father, took the treasure away to the wilderness and there hoarded it. And there he stayed, taking on the form of a dragon, until Regin contrived his death.

Shaw's 'perfect Wagnerite' will recognise some of this, at any rate in outline: a golden treasure, a ring that is accursed, got by treachery from a dwarf; a body to be covered with gold, and a ring that must be piled on to complete the process. The prologue to *Der Ring des Nibelungen*, *Das Rheingold*, has reflections also of myths told earlier in this book: a stronghold for the gods built by giants under a contract that is to be renounced; a goddess who keeps the apples of youth and who is seized by giants with the result that the gods become aged and wan. Clearly Wagner derived a good deal of his matter from Norse myth, adapting it to his own intellectual purposes. Yet much of Wagner's music drama is taken up with the adventures of two heroes, father and son, Siegmund and Siegfried, whose ambiguous relationship to the gods and particularly to Odin (Wagner's W*otan*) leads to disaster.

Norse tradition too shows this connection between the myth of the cursed ring and a family of hero-kings. I say 'Norse tradition' but in fact the material is essentially central European rather than Norse, though it is the literature of medieval Scandinavia that preserves it most completely. Behind the legendary names that the Norse writers record, certain historical characters can be discerned. The king called *Gunnarr* was probably the *Gundaharius* of the fifth-century Burgundian dynasty, while the villainous *Atli* is a reflection of the ferocious Hunnish leader *Attila* who died in 451. The king *Iǫrmunrekr* represents *Ermanaric*, the fourth-century king of the Ostro-Goths, while *Hiálprekr* may be the sixth-century Merovingian *Chilperic*. The order in which these characters appear in the Scandinavian cycle defies chronology.

The Norse legends are related in a group of heroic poems of the *Poetic Edda*. Though I call them a group, they diverge widely in date and form. Some are probably from quite early in the Viking Age, others as late as the twelfth century. Some are straightforward narrative verse, broken by stanzas of dialogue. Others have verse narrative and speech interspersed with sections of narrative prose, and the relationship between verse and prose passages has led to discussion and indeed controversy. Others again tell a story from the standpoint of one of its characters, looking back upon past events. For all their variety, there is a good deal of similarity of content and theme: their events are fierce feuds, carried on by kings of cruel temperament, often assisted by women of equal ferocity. Kings are arrogant, often avaricious, eager for glory or afraid of seeming cowardly. The general atmosphere is pagan, as all Christians will readily confirm.

Part of the whole tale Snorri recorded in his *Prose Edda*. More important for the complete narrative is the version in *Vǫlsunga saga*, a prose re-telling from the thirteenth century, extant in one early manuscript from *c.*1400. In essence *Vǫlsunga saga* reproduces the Eddic poems, linking them into one continuous story, and also preserving material from sources that no longer exist. The effect is sometimes inconsistent, for the poems do not always tell identical stories. In addition there are minor Norse sources (including Saxo Grammaticus), a very considerable amount of information in medieval German works – though some of this diverges from the Norse – and even brief references from Anglo-Saxon England showing that at any rate parts of the legend were known there.

The Scandinavian version begins with a king called Volsung, the founder of a great dynasty in Hunland, thought to be descended from Odin. He begot ten sons and a daughter, though only one son, Sigmund, and his twin sister, Signy, are named. Volsung was a tough king and a fine warrior, and kept great state in a splendid hall which had a tree growing in its midst. A powerful king, Siggeir of Gautland (Götaland, Sweden), wooed Signy, and a marriage was arranged. Naturally there was a great wedding feast. As all were seated round the central fires, in came an unknown figure, an old man, one-eyed, wearing a cape and with his face covered with a hood. Who could it be but Odin, though nobody recognised him? He was carrying a sword. He plunged it into the tree's trunk and announced that the man who could pull it out again could keep it. Then off he went. All the guests tried to pull the sword out, but only Sigmund succeeded. When they examined the weapon, everyone agreed it was the finest sword ever seen. Siggeir wanted to buy it, but Sigmund refused, and so ill-will grew between the families. (The sword in the tree motif recurs, of course, in Wagner's *Die Walküre*.)

Siggeir cut the wedding feast short and returned home, taking Signy with him much against her will. However, Siggeir had given Volsung and his sons a return invitation to visit Gautland in three months' time. When Volsung arrived there, he found Siggeir with an army mustered against him. His pride would not let him retreat, though he was now advanced in years. So they joined battle. Despite a valiant resistance, Volsung and all his men were killed, only the ten sons surviving as captives.

At Signy's suggestion they were chained to a log in the middle of the woods and left there. Each night a she-wolf came from her lair and ate one of the sons until Sigmund alone was left. At this rather late point Signy had a brainwave. She sent her servant with a jar of honey, which he smeared all over Sigmund's face and into his mouth. When the wolf arrived as usual, she sniffed the honey and began to lick Sigmund's face; at last she put her tongue into his mouth to get the honey. Sigmund bit into the wolf's tongue, and she jumped back, straining with her feet at the log so that it cracked in pieces. Sigmund bit on her tongue so that it tore from its roots. The wolf it was that died.

So Sigmund became free, and hid in the woods with Signy's connivance. There the pair plotted revenge. Signy sent her two sons to see if they could help her brother, but they proved feeble so Sigmund killed them off. Strangely enough Siggeir seems not to have noticed their disappearance. Signy decided she must have a son by her brother if he were to be tough enough to help in the act of vengeance. So she changed shapes with a comely witch, visited her brother and slept with him. From this union a son, Sinfiotli, was born; and a very harsh character he turned out to be. (The incestuous coupling that results in the birth of a hero is also reflected in *Die Walküre*.)

Father and son had a spell of battle training, and then made their way to Siggeir's hall, hiding in the entrance lobby. There Signy's latest two children spotted them, so Sinfiotli sliced them up with his sword and threw the remains into the hall. Even the lethargic Siggeir reacted at this, ordering the intruders to be seized. After the usual gallant resistance Sigmund and Sinfiotli were taken, and buried alive in a turf mound so that they would die in protracted agony. But Signy threw a piece of meat into the mound before it was closed up. When they examined it they found there was a sword stuck into the joint. Between them they sawed their way out of the mound, set fire to Siggeir's hall and burnt him alive. Signy refused to leave her husband, realising that her behaviour could not allow escape. So she died with him.

This ferocious tale has no extant source, though its origin is implied in a bit of verse quoted to illustrate the two kinsmen's escape from the mound. As the verse says:

> With strength they cut the massive slab,
> Sigmund with his sword and Sinfiotli.

Apparently here as elsewhere the author of *Vǫlsunga saga* has turned a poem he knew (but which hasn't come down to us) into rather pedestrian prose.

Sigmund and his son/nephew shipped themselves back to his ancestral lands, and Sigmund took power there, marrying a woman Borghild and having by her two sons, one of whom, Helgi, was to become famous. So ends the first episode in the Volsung story.

Vǫlsunga saga's second section reports the adventures of Helgi and his uncle Sinfiotli. It derives in part from an Eddic poem, *The first lay of Helgi Hunding's Killer*, which we can supplement from the more complex material of a second lay on that hero. As a young man Helgi went on a freebooting expedition with Sinfiotli, and attacked and killed a king called Hunding. Hunding's sons took exception, and when Helgi refused to pay them blood-money, they called up an army and fought him. They were beaten, and several lost their lives. Returning from the battle Helgi met a party of women, one of whom was a king's daughter Sigrun. By profession she was a valkyrie. She complained she was being given in marriage to a weakling, King Hoddbrodd, and Helgi volunteered to save her from this dread fate. He brought his force to Hoddbrodd's land where the home guard were awaiting them. After a disgraceful scene of mutual insult between the leaders of the two armies, Helgi attacked and destroyed his enemy with the assistance of Sigrun's valkyries. Helgi settled down with Sigrun and is heard of no more in the *Vǫlsunga saga*, though the second lay relates his death at the hands of an avenger.

Sinfiotli continued his piracy and met up with an attractive woman who was also being courted by Borghild's brother. Sinfiotli struck his rival down. Returning, he was surprised to find he was unwelcome to Borghild. Sigmund insisted that Sinfiotli should remain with them. Borghild prepared her brother's wake, with a splendid feast. As was the custom, she served the drink and took a full horn to Sinfiotli. He thought the liquor cloudy and wouldn't drink: so Sigmund finished it off. But then, Sigmund could drink poison without taking harm; Sinfiotli couldn't. Borghild brought a second round. 'The drink has been tampered with', said Sinfiotli. Again Sigmund drank it off. Borghild tried a third time. 'There's poison in this drink', said Sinfiotli. By now Sigmund was drunk and incapable of judgment. 'Strain it through your moustache then', he advised. Sinfiotli did and fell down dead. Sigmund, broken with grief, took the body to the shore of the fiord where he came upon a man (could this be Odin again?) with a boat so small it would take only one passenger. Sigmund loaded the body on to the boat and prepared to walk round the fiord side; but as he did, the boat vanished. Sigmund returned home and banished his vengeful queen who died soon after.

Sigmund married again, a king's daughter Hiordis. His unsuccessful rival in love was one of Hunding's sons, Lyngvi. Lyngvi felt this was the last straw and resolved to destroy Sigmund. He invaded Hunland and offered battle. There was a tough fight, with Sigmund, now an old man, defending himself courageously. In the midst of the strife appeared a man, one-eyed, with a black cloak and floppy hat, and carrying a spear (Odin!). The man stood in Sigmund's path with his spear aloft. Sigmund's sword shattered against the spear, and at that the battle turned against the defenders and Sigmund was mortally wounded. (A similar occurrence is in *Die Walküre.*)

The pregnant Hiordis had been put in a place of safety in the woods, with all the royal treasure. She went out to seek among the wounded, finding Sigmund in his death agonies. Sigmund prophesied the greatness of the son who would be born to them, and instructed Hiordis to preserve the fragments of his sword for the child's benefit. Thereupon he died, and Hiordis was taken into the protection of a group of passing Vikings led by the king of Denmark's son.

Vǫlsunga saga's third section relates the exploits of Hiordis's son by Sigmund. This was to be the greatest of Germanic heroes, Sigurd (Wagner's *Siegfried*). It is here that the heroic legend of the Volsungs links to the god myth of the great gold treasure with its fatal ring. Sigurd was fostered with honour in the king of Denmark's court. His tutor there was the smith Regin, disaffected brother of Fafnir, now a dragon guarding his stolen wealth. Regin taught Sigurd accomplishments suited to a prince, but also tried to make him discontented with his position as a dependent at court. 'Who was looking after Sigurd's rightful royal inheritance?' 'The Danish king and his son.' But did Sigurd trust them? Did they treat him generously enough? Why didn't he have his own horse?

Sigurd replied he could have a horse – or anything else he wanted – for the asking. The king gave him freedom to choose from his stud. When Sigurd went to pick out the best horse, he met an old bearded man otherwise unknown to him. We are not told the man was one-eyed, but we may suspect it. Obviously Odin. The stranger advised Sigurd how to select a horse and between them they chose one that Sleipnir had sired (and so must have admirable qualities). They named it Grani.

Next Regin put into Sigurd's mind the desire for money, saying he knew where there was treasure for the taking. A dragon called Fafnir guarded it, and had its lair on a heath not far off. But Sigurd would need a sword to kill the monster with. Regin forged the lad a sword, but when the hero chopped at an anvil with it, the blade shattered. Regin made a second, better one. It smashed just like the first. Sigurd went to his mother and asked for the bits of his father's sword that she had kept by her all these years. With this metal, obviously skilfully balanced, Regin made a new blade, so tough it would slice through an anvil, yet so sharp it would cut a strand of wool drifting down the river. Before attacking the dragon, Sigurd mounted an expedition against his father's killers and destroyed them. Now he was ready for Fafnir.

With Regin he went up on to the heath and traced the tracks Fafnir made when he went to his watering hole. They were enormous and made Sigurd apprehensive. Regin advised him to dig a pit along the track so that when the dragon crawled to the water, he could lurk in it and stab the beast in the soft underbelly. Sigurd prepared his trap, but was interrupted by an old man (who could it be?) who advised him to dig a row of pits so that the dragon's blood would flow into them and do Sigurd no harm. Sigurd took this advice, and struck Fafnir his death-blow. The Eddic poem *Fáfnismál*, the Tale of Fafnir, records the exchanges between the dying Fafnir and his victor. These include warnings to the lad of the fate the treasure would bring him:

'The ringing gold, the glow-red treasure,
The rings will bring you to your death.'

Sigurd was unmoved:

'For every man in fullness of time
Must descend to his death.'

When the monster was safely despatched, Regin came up, cut out its heart and drank some of its blood. Then he asked Sigurd to roast the heart for him. Sigurd spitted it on a stake which he held over a fire. When it looked ready and juice was frothing out of it, Sigurd felt it with his finger to test if it was properly done. The meat was hot, and Sigurd popped his finger into his mouth to cool it. The moment Fafnir's blood came on to his tongue, he found he could understand the language of birds. Above him in a tree perched a flock of nuthatches, twittering together. One said:

'There sits Sigurd spattered with blood.
He's brazing Fafnir's heart on the fire.
That ring-scatterer [prince] would seem wiser to me
If he ate the glittering serpent's heart.'

Other birds joined in, revealing Regin's intended treachery to the lad, and suggesting Sigurd should lop off the smith's head, take all the riches to himself and go off and learn wisdom from the valkyrie Brynhild who lay in a charmed sleep on Hind Fell. Sigurd approved this advice, drew his sword and beheaded Regin. He ate some of the dragon's heart, and kept the rest for future use, leaped on his horse Grani and traced Fafnir's tracks to his lair. There he

All the Sigurd carvings illustrated opposite
are on the doorway from Hylestad church,
Oldsaksamling, Oslo, Norway.
TOP LEFT Sigurd, the right-hand figure, tests
his sword to destruction. Regin looks on
crossly. MIDDLE LEFT Regin and his helper
forge another new sword from the fragments
of Sigmund's blade. BOTTOM LEFT Sigurd
stabs the dragon in the belly.
TOP RIGHT Regin sleeps while Sigurd
roasts Fafnir's heart and tests it to see if it's
ready. As he tastes the blood, he understands
the speech of the birds in the trees above him.
MIDDLE RIGHT Sigurd follows the
birds' advice and kills off Regin. BOTTOM
RIGHT Sigurd's horse Grani, loaded with
treasure acquired from Fafnir the dragon.

A runic memorial inscription (right) set
within a snake-like form. The carver took the
snake to be Fafnir, and carved Sigurd
beneath, stabbing the dragon in the belly.

found more treasures than two or three ordinary horses could carry; yet he
loaded them all on Grani, sprang into the saddle and rode away.

This is the point where Sigurd's affairs, hitherto fairly straightforward,
become tangled, for he found himself involved with two strong-minded
women, Brynhild and Gudrun, his future bride. There is also a confusion
of traditions: it is not easy to derive a simple story from the various sources.
Vǫlsunga saga tells how Sigurd rode up on to Hind Fell, and saw in the
distance a blazing fire. When he came closer, he found it surrounded a fortress.
Within lay an armoured figure fast asleep. Sigurd slit open the armour –
his sword cut metal as if it were cloth – and found it was a woman, the
valkyrie Brynhild whom Odin had put to sleep for disobedience. Sigurd woke
her and was entranced by her beauty and intelligence. He fell for her and
she for him, and they swore mutual faith.

Then follows a confusion in the tale. Sigurd rode away (why?) and came
to the home of Heimir, Brynhild's foster-father, where his splendid appearance
caused a sensation. Brynhild was now staying at Heimir's (how did she get
there?), and again Sigurd made his profession of love to her. This time she
was apprehensive, for she was a valkyrie, happy when leading a battle-force.
He was fated to marry Gudrun, Giuki's daughter. Sigurd denied this would
happen, and again he and Brynhild swore vows of devotion. Sigurd gave
her a gold ring: indeed, the gold ring.

And so to the hall of Giuki, south of the Rhine. Giuki had a wife, the
witch Grimhild, three sons, Gunnar, Hogni and Guttorm, and a daughter
Gudrun. Brynhild was Gudrun's friend, and the two consulted about the
future. Brynhild interpreted Gudrun's dreams, foretelling her unhappy fate:
she would marry Sigurd and lose him.

Sigurd reached Giuki's hall with all his treasure. Giuki welcomed him in, and Grimhild soon recognised that Sigurd would be a great asset to the family. If only he were not in love with Brynhild. Grimhild solved the problem by giving Sigurd an enchanted drink that made him forget his old love. To retain Sigurd's support, Giuki offered him the hand of his daughter Gudrun, and Sigurd, blissfully oblivious of Brynhild, accepted. They had a splendid wedding, and to bind the alliance, Gunnar, Hogni and Sigurd swore blood-brotherhood. After that the men of the family went off a-pirating, and returned home rich with plunder. Sigurd gave Gudrun some of Fafnir's heart to eat, 'and after that she was much crueller than before, as well as wiser'.

Meanwhile Gunnar was getting restless for a bit of married life. He decided to court Brynhild, and Sigurd agreed to help. She would marry only the man who rode through the encircling fire to her hall, and Gunnar tried to do it. His horse shied away and wouldn't enter the flame. Gunnar asked to borrow Grani, but even Grani wouldn't go on with Gunnar up. So Sigurd and Gunnar exchanged appearances (how, I wonder), and Sigurd mounted Grani and charged through the flames. Within her hall sat Brynhild, majestic in armour and helmet. Sigurd/Gunnar announced that he had ridden the fire and was entitled to her hand. She accepted, welcoming him to her home and her bed. Sigurd/Gunnar laid his drawn sword between them as they slept. Then he took back the great gold ring, exchanging it for another. There-after he rode back through the flames and the two friends changed into their own guises. A great wedding feast was held for Brynhild and Gunnar, and now, when it was too late, Sigurd remembered his meeting with Brynhild. But he made no sign.

Shortly afterwards Gudrun and Brynhild had a quarrel over precedence. Brynhild claimed her husband was the greater, as he had ridden through the ring of fire to her. Gudrun revealed what had really happened, that it was Sigurd in Gunnar's guise who had ridden the flame wall, and she had the great ring to prove it. Brynhild went white with anger and plotted ven-geance on Sigurd and Gudrun, the man and woman who had shamed her, and on Gunnar, the husband who had taken her by deceit. Sigurd's soft answers could not turn away her wrath.

Brynhild spoke to her husband, warning him of the danger of having so eminent a fighter as Sigurd in his household:

'Back shall I go where I used to be,
Living together with my father's kin.
There will I sit and sleep my life away
Unless you make sure of Sigurd's death,
Unless you become a prince greater than all others.'

Gunnar was now in a tricky position. He could not harm Sigurd for they were bloodbrothers, yet he would like the treasure to be his. Hogni could not attack Sigurd either; indeed he felt more engaged by his oath than Gunnar was. Then Gunnar had a bright idea. Why not get their young brother Guttorm to do the killing – he was not involved in the compact? The two brothers urged Guttorm to the murder, offering him money and power. They gave him enchanted food (which sounds distinctly unpalatable) to charm him. Grimhild added her persuasions, and Guttorm fell.

Sigurd was lying abed, unsuspecting. Guttorm went twice to his room, but Sigurd was awake and his looks so terrifying that Guttorm ran off in panic. But on the third occasion Sigurd slept, and Guttorm thrust him through with his sword. Sigurd awoke at the blow, grabbed for his sword and threw it at Guttorm as he escaped through the doorway. It sliced him through at the waist, and half fell back into the room, half out. Gudrun, who had been asleep in Sigurd's arms, awoke drenched with blood, and her grief was uncontrolled. Sigurd died, accusing Brynhild of responsibility for the deed, but recognising it had long been fated to happen. When Brynhild heard Gudrun's bitter moan of misery, she laughed aloud. Then she made Gunnar understand the implications of the killing: now the brothers would not have Sigurd's support when they rode into battle. As they prepared Sigurd's burial, Brynhild stabbed herself, and begged to be put on the funeral pyre with him, with the drawn sword lying between them as it had done so long ago. So ended the great hero, after a life of peril, glory and treachery. (Wagnerites will recognise much of the plots of *Siegfried* and *Götterdämmerung* here.)

The last sections of *Vǫlsunga saga* relate the terrible fate of Gudrun after her husband's death. For a time she hid in the wilderness, and then lived in exile in Denmark. There her brothers found her, and brought compensation for her ills. Grimhild produced another of her enchanted drinks that made Gudrun forget her wrongs. Then, with doubtful tact, they betrothed her to Atli, Brynhild's brother, much against her will. Atli coveted the treasure that Sigurd had left, and which was now in the brothers' power. He invited Gunnar and Hogni to visit him, intending treachery. Gudrun tried to warn them, but failed; the brothers were seduced by the possibility of inheriting Atli's kingdom. So they went. When they disembarked in Atli's territory, the treachery was revealed, but Gunnar and Hogni rode boldly to Atli's hall. There they fought a pitched battle against Atli's men, and when their sister saw them hard pressed she took sword and armour and joined in on their side. There was terrible slaughter, but in the end Gunnar and Hogni were captured and put in chains.

Gunnar was made an offer. He could save his life if he revealed where the hoard was hidden. 'Let me see my brother Hogni's heart cut out of his body first.' But Atli's men cut out the heart of a cowardly slave and showed it to Gunnar as Hogni's. Gunnar didn't believe it. The heart was quivering in terror as Hogni's never did. So they cut out Hogni's heart, and he laughed scornfully the while. They took the heart to Gunnar and he recognised it. 'Only I know where the gold is now Hogni cannot tell you. I was in doubt while we both lived, but now I alone have the decision. The Rhine shall hold that gold before Huns wear it on their arms.'

Atli put Gunnar in a pit with poisonous snakes. His hands were bound,

Gunnar lies bound in the snake-pit, trying to charm the snakes. It avails him little. Also on the doorway from Hylestad church, Oldsaksamling, Oslo, Norway.

but Gudrun threw a harp into the pit, and he charmed the serpents by playing to them with his toes. However, in the end a venomous adder dug its fangs into him and he died.

Both Atli and Gudrun had friends to mourn, so they arranged a joint wake in reconciliation, or so Atli thought. For the feast Gudrun served up the hearts of her sons by Atli, mixed their blood with the festive wine and fashioned their skulls into drinking cups. Thereafter she and one of Hogni's sons stabbed Atli and set fire to his hall. There is no doubt that eating dragon's heart will bring out the worst in a woman.

Yet Gudrun's griefs were still not complete. Her lovely daughter Svanhild was betrothed to the elderly King Iormunrek. He suspected her of infidelity and had her trampled beneath his horses' hooves. Avenging her, Gudrun's surviving sons took Iormunrek in his hall and chopped off his arms and legs. Before they could kill him he shouted to his men to stone his assailants to death, and so they perished. But by that time, according to Snorri, Fafnir's inheritance, the cursed gold, had been hidden in the River Rhine. 'And it has never been found since.' □

Suggestions for further reading

The study of Norse myths is a complex business, and this book can only simplify it. Even the sources I describe are more complicated than I make them out to be – there are variant readings of texts, and variant translations and interpretations. All I have tried to do here is draw a general picture. Those who want to know more have access to a full and authoritative translation of Snorri's *Edda* in A. Faulkes, *Snorri Sturluson: Edda* (London, 1987). This is excellent in its accuracy and closeness to the original but in consequence loses in fluency and readability: nevertheless it is much to be commended. There is no equivalent translation of the *Poetic Edda* though there have been many attempts. Most recently W. H. Auden and P. B. Taylor compiled *Norse poems* (London, 1981). This has most of the Eddic verse in it, though the treatment is often idiosyncratic as in their reorganisation of *Hávamál*. For a text of that most important poem it is perhaps best to go to the rather antique version and translation, D. E. Martin Clarke, *The Hávamál* (Cambridge, 1923). You may come upon attempts at the full *Poetic Edda* by H. A. Bellows and L. M. Hollander, though neither is very distinguished.

The verses of the skalds are hard to come by in translation, partly because of the fearsome problems of rendering their language and construction into readable English. Some of the poems I mention, together with a competent introduction, are in E. O. G. Turville-Petre, *Scaldic poetry* (Oxford, 1976). The text of *Ynglingasaga* can be found in L. M. Hollander's translation of *Heimskringla: history of the kings of Norway* (Austin, Texas, 1964), and there is also a convenient Everyman's Library edition, rather old-fashioned but re-issued fairly recently. A very useful translation of Saxo Grammaticus's *Gesta Danorum* has appeared, the relevant early part being *Saxo Grammaticus: the history of the Danes*, vol. 1, translated by Peter Fisher (Cambridge, 1979). A good text, with translation and introduction, of *Volsunga saga* is R. G. Finch, *The saga of the Volsungs* (Nelson's Icelandic Texts, Edinburgh and London, 1965), while U. Dronke's *The Poetic Edda*, vol. 1, *Heroic Poems* (Oxford, 1969), gives the four poems whose material provides the later episodes of that saga, with a translation that sometimes makes them sound more poetic than they really are.

A good introduction to the modern study of Norse mythology is in the first chapter, 'Mythology and mythography', in C. J. Clover and J. Lindow, *Old Norse-Icelandic literature: a critical guide* (Cornell, Ithaca, 1985). Other chapters are helpful in giving the literary background to much of what I say here. For an up-to-date summary of the relevant medieval literature there is J. Kristjánsson, *Eddas and sagas*, translated by P. Foote (Reykjavík, 1988). The reader of German should turn to the standard work, J. de Vries, *Altgermanische Religionsgeschichte*, second edition, 2 vols (Berlin, 1957). In English perhaps the best available general work on Norse mythology is still E. O. G. Turville-Petre, *Myth and religion of the north: the religion of ancient Scandinavia* (London, 1964), useful despite being marred by numerous literal misprints and inconsistencies. For those reluctant to read French, Georges Dumézil's views can be found, though not criticised, in the English translation, *Gods of the ancient Northmen*, edited by E. Haugen (Berkeley and Los Angeles, 1973). □

Index and picture credits

Picture credits

Photographs have been supplied by courtesy of the following: *front cover, pp. 9, 12, 19 (right), 29*: British Museum Publications, London; *pp. 45, 64 (right)*: Professor R. Cramp, University of Durham; *p. 75*: Bernt A. Lundberg, Statens Historiska Museum, Stockholm; *p. 11 (bottom)*: The Manx Museum and National Trust, Douglas; *pp. 74 (all), 78*: Dr Sue Margeson, Castle Museum, Norwich; *pp. 8 (right), 11 (top)*: Nationalmuseet, Copenhagen; *p. 13*: National Museum of Iceland, Reykjavik; *p. 64 (left)*: Oldsaksamlingen, Universiteti Oslo; *p. 51 (left)* Royal Commission on the Historical Monuments of England *pp. 4–5*: Jan Slot-Carlsen, Aalborg Historiske Museum; *pp. 8 (left), 21*: Statens Historiska Museum, Stockholm; *p. 19 (left)*: Uppsala University Library.